LATER ISLAMIC POTTERY
PERSIA, SYRIA, EGYPT, TURKEY

The Faber Monographs on Pottery and Porcelain

Former Editors: W. B. HONEY and ARTHUR LANE
Present Editors: SIR HARRY GARNER and R. J. CHARLESTON

*

*F. Turkish (Isnik); about 1570–80. Ht. 10 in.
Victoria and Albert Museum. (pages 57, 58)*

LATER ISLAMIC POTTERY
PERSIA, SYRIA, EGYPT, TURKEY

by

ARTHUR LANE

FABER AND FABER
3 Queen Square
London

First published in 1957
by Faber and Faber Limited
Second edition 1971
Printed in Great Britain by
R. MacLehose and Company Limited
The University Press Glasgow
All rights reserved

ISBN 0 571 04736 X

FOREWORD
TO SECOND EDITION (1971)

For this second edition the text has been revised by Ralph Pinder-Wilson, Deputy Keeper in the Department of Oriental Antiquities at the British Museum, and a number of fresh bibliographical references have been added. Four new colour plates enrich the illustration of the pottery dealt with in the book, reliant as it is on colour for its full effect.

R.J.C.

CONTENTS

CONTENTS

ILLUSTRATIONS

COLOUR PLATES

MONOCHROME PLATES
at the end of the book

ix

ILLUSTRATIONS

AUTHOR'S ACKNOWLEDGEMENTS

It would be difficult to name individually all the friends and colleagues who have generously given help of various kinds during the many years spent in collecting material for this book. But special thanks are due, among private collectors, to Sir Alan Barlow, Lt.-Col. R. H. Brocklebank, the Misses Godman, and Mr. Gerald Reitlinger. I have learnt much in discussion with Professor Ernst Kühnel, the doyen of Islamic art studies; with Dr. L. A. Mayer of Jerusalem; Professor Kurt Erdmann of Istanbul; Dr. Richard Ettinghausen of the Freer Gallery, Washington; Dr. Mohamed Mostafa of the Museum of Islamic Art, Cairo; and Dr. D. S. Rice of the University of London. My colleague John Ayers at the Victoria and Albert Museum has helped in Chinese matters, and I here acknowledge the use of many of the Museum's official photographs. Other photographs have kindly been made available by the British Museum; the Musée du Louvre and Musée des Arts Décoratifs, Paris; the Staatliche Museen, Berlin; the Rijksmuseum, Amsterdam; Dr. Vagn Poulsen of the Ny Carlsberg Glyptothek, Copenhagen; the Hermitage Museum, Leningrad; the Topkapu Sarayi Müzesi, Istanbul; and the Metropolitan Museum of Art, New York.

ACKNOWLEDGEMENTS (1971)

Thanks are due to the Victoria and Albert Museum, the British Museum, the Metropolitan Museum of Art, New York, and the Keir Collection for permission to reproduce material in the second edition.

INTRODUCTION

This book is a sequel, in the same series, to *Early Islamic Pottery* (1947), an account of the fine wares made in the Near East from the ninth century A.D. till about 1300. The medieval wares as a whole represented one of the great creative movements in the potter's art. Their makers had begun with a bare minimum of skill inherited from antiquity, and a desire to emulate the much-prized porcelain and stoneware that had newly arrived from China. But the Islamic potters had no access to hard-firing clays of the Chinese kind, and as if to repair this deficiency, they showed infinite resource in devising new ceramic techniques—particularly those in which coloured glazes were combined with painted or incised decoration. Fundamentally different methods were pursued in various regions of the Islamic world. In Mesopotamia during the ninth and tenth centuries, and in Egypt under Fātimid rule, the type preferred was a fine buff earthenware with an opaque white glaze, over which painting was added in 'gold lustre'. The contemporary potters of Eastern Persia and Turkestan painted their earthenware with coloured clay 'slips' under a transparent lead-glaze. Similar materials were used, especially in Persia, for many varieties of 'sgraffiato' ware, in which designs were incised through a white slip ground to show the darker clay underneath. With the twelfth century came a revolution in technique which spread throughout the Near East. In place of the red or buff clay, a translucent white composition, akin to the later European 'soft-paste' porcelain, was universally adopted for wares of fine quality. With its associated alkaline glaze, it has remained the standard material of Near Eastern pottery till modern times, but it has never since been handled with a skill equal to that of the Persian potters of the twelfth and thirteenth centuries.

Masters of their own technique, the medieval Islamic potters could draw fully on the stock of designs they shared with artists working in other materials. In its early stages Islamic art had been a fusion of surviving Greco-Roman naturalism with the more ponderous heraldic style bequeathed by Sasanian Persia. The naturalism lost its illusion of a third dimension, and the heraldic motives failed to maintain their separate identity; both merged into a strongly rhythmic system that could be logically extended to cover a flat surface of any shape. The

xiii

'arabesque' complex tends to move away from the naturalism of the living plant to the abstraction of pure geometry, but always preserves the sense of being an organic whole. Human and animal figures had their place in early Islamic art, but only as subordinate parts of the decorative system; they were supported, or rather half-submerged, by the coiling stems and leaves of the arabesque. Their emotive import- ance was far less than that of the ornamental Arabic inscriptions whose presence was a perpetual reminder of the Koran, and whose calli- graphic elegance prescribed the tone of all the other decoration.

It should be emphasized that the art of these medieval Islamic potters, so superbly articulate, was without parallel in the ancient or contemporary world. The Chinese wares of the T'ang and Sung dynas- ties surpassed them in other respects, but in painted design the Islamic wares were still supreme. In Christian Europe pottery was then a neglected craft, and outside the Byzantine Empire even the use of rudimentary ceramic glazes remained exceptional throughout the Middle Ages.

A date about 1300 is a convenient point at which to divide 'early' from 'late' Islamic pottery for the purpose of study. The Mongol in- vasions, which began in 1219, almost paralysed the cultural life of Persia. The famous potteries of Rayy and Raqqa succumbed to the Mongol attack; and though the kilns of Kāshān continued active into the fourteenth century, they were by then working in an outmoded style and technique. In 1295 the Mongols at last formally adopted the religion of their Persian subjects and sponsored a revival of the civil- ized arts. But it soon became apparent that something had changed; even the new pottery was quite different in spirit from the old, and the new ceramic styles quickly spread from Persia to other parts of the Islamic world. It is possible to make certain generalizations about the Islamic wares of the five centuries after 1300. They are far less various in technique than the wares of the Middle Ages. Only the relatively rough products of provincial or village potters were henceforward made in earthenware; anything of artistic pretension was made in the white composite paste. This material itself was generally softer, and always less sensitively handled than in the twelfth and thirteenth centuries, when it was still a new discovery; the shapes of the vessels therefore rarely showed much subtlety of profile. The costly processes of overglaze-painting in 'gold lustre' and enamel colours practically died out during the fourteenth century (though lustre was revived on a small class of seventeenth-century Persian wares). There remained the cheaper method of underglaze-painting, which needed only a single firing. A new and completer range of underglaze colours was introduced in the Turkish and Persian wares of the sixteenth century.

INTRODUCTION

The decoration on the later Islamic wares is often admirable, but fails on the whole to maintain the astonishing force and originality so constantly present in wares of medieval date. For this there were probably deep-seated reasons. Islamic civilization suffered severe set-backs in the thirteenth century; in addition to their wholesale destruction of human life and property, the Mongols had exterminated the line of the Abbasid Caliphs, and thenceforward the Muslim faith had no generally recognized spiritual leader. The Islamic countries failed to keep pace with the growing economic power of Christian Europe, whose explorers were soon discovering routes along which to harvest the riches of the earth. There was no Islamic counterpart to the European Renaissance; an ageing civilization had no stimulus to reshape its intellectual life, or to create a new language in art. In the first few centuries after the conquests the artist had known how to impart to his arabesque something of the spiritual tension found in the early Arabic scripts; the fervour of the Islamic faith was implicit in his work. But from the fourteenth century onwards the arabesque tends to become over-elaborate or tamely academic, and then to disintegrate. A cold archaism invades the decorative inscriptions, or they are so perfunctorily written as to be meaningless; in later Islamic art they tend to disappear altogether. The brilliant schools of Persian miniature-painting developed with a predominantly secular tone. Exotic flora and fauna taken over from Chinese art found a place beside the arabesques, with which their modified naturalism was not in keeping: this hybrid style is well seen on the animal-carpets made in Persia under the Safavids. In pottery it was even harder to maintain the integrity of an Islamic style than in the other arts. For the Chinese had at last begun to cover their wares with painted decoration, in a technique which the Islamic potters could easily compass; and it was far easier to imitate the mannered Chinese subjects literally, colour-scheme and all, than to abstract and assimilate a few ideas that could be transformed into a convincingly Islamic idiom. In the seventeenth century the Persian potters were even more under the spell of Chinese blue-and-white than their European contemporaries at Delft, Frankfurt, and Nevers. But it can at least be said that the Persian imitations were superior to the European in technique and in the genuinely oriental, if not strictly Chinese, touch of their painting.

It is a paradox that there are gaps in our knowledge of the later Islamic wares, more serious than in the case of their medieval predecessors. The latter are 'archaeological' material, found by excavation on the sites of medieval cities such as Rayy and Raqqa, which have lain abandoned since the Mongol invasions; and in the last eighty years much excavation has been done. A good deal of later pottery, on the other hand, has survived above ground since the day it was made. We have much Turkish pottery of the sixteenth and seventeenth centuries, and Persian wares of the seventeenth and eighteenth. But far more of the material evidence we need still lies broken and buried, awaiting the excavator's spade. We know practically nothing about Persian pottery of the fifteenth century, and would be almost equally ignorant of the sixteenth-century wares, had not many pieces of one particular class been preserved as house-ornaments in a remote Caucasian village outside the confines of Persia. It would in fact be difficult to organize an archaeological search for these wares, for the places where they must have been made have since remained in continuous occupation, and the kilns probably lie buried under modern buildings. Moreover, most excavations in Persia hitherto have been financed by antique-dealers, less concerned with archaeological evidence than with the prospect of selling the finds to western collectors and museums. The latter, for their part, have not so far been interested in spending money on damaged Near Eastern wares of post-medieval date, when better-preserved Chinese and European pottery of the same period has been available for them to collect. The fine Turkish pottery and tiles of Isnik, of which plenty survive in good condition, have long been cherished by collectors—their superb decorative qualities could hardly be ignored. But the late Persian wares have not been appreciated as they deserve, perhaps partly because they are so little understood. The whole range of later Islamic wares may today be better studied in the great museums of Europe and the United States than in the Near East. The collections in the Victoria and Albert Museum are unrivalled, thanks to private benefactions and prudent purchases in the last century.

1

THE FOURTEENTH-CENTURY
MONGOL STYLE

General

Besieged by the Crusaders from the west and the Mongols from the
east, Islamic civilization in the thirteenth century narrowly escaped
final disaster. Defeat by the Christians at Las Navas de Tolosa in 1212
hastened the downfall of Moslem Spain. Egypt was invaded in 1218–
1221, and again by St. Louis in 1249; Syrian Antioch remained a
Crusader stronghold till 1268. But the danger from the east was
incomparably greater.

By 1206 the nomad barbarian tribes of Mongolia had been united
into a confederacy under Jenghiz Khan. It is said that fifty million
people lost their lives in the campaigns led by Jenghiz and his successors—the threefold expansion of the Mongol Empire into China,
Western Asia, and Russia. China was always the main front. Here the
Tartar Chin dynasty of the north was conquered between 1211 and
1234; the native Sung dynasty of the south in stages lasting till 1279.
Kubilai Khan on his accession in 1260 moved his capital from Karakorum in Mongolia to Cambaluc (Peking), where he and his line ruled
as Yüan Emperors of China (1280–1368).

The westward operations of the Mongols had at first the character
of devastating raids, from which most of the invaders returned with
their plunder into Central Asia. Transoxiana and Persia were thus
overrun between 1219 and 1224, and a force branching off through
the Caucasus made in 1221 the first attack on Russia. The main thrust
against Russia followed between 1236 and 1241, when the Mongols
under Batu, passing north of the Caspian Sea, penetrated into Eastern
Europe as far as Poland and Hungary. From these thinly populated
areas they soon retired, but they established a great armed camp at
Sarai on the Volga, whence Batu and his successors of the 'Golden
Horde' dominated the Christian princes of Russia till the fifteenth
century.

LATER ISLAMIC POTTERY

We are here most concerned with the Mongols in Persia. Not until 1252 was a permanent ruler designated for this region in the person of Hulagu, a grandson of Jenghiz and the founder of the Persian Il-Khan dynasty (1256–1336). His instructions were to break the power of Islam, the soul of resistance to the Mongols, and to carry their conquests further west. In 1258 Hulagu's troops captured and destroyed Baghdad, where they put to death the Caliph Mu'tasim and the 'Abbāsid family which for five centuries had been honoured as the spiritual leaders of Islam. From Baghdad the Mongols passed on into Syria, where they took Aleppo and Damascus and destroyed Raqqa. But in 1260, at 'Ayn Jālūt (the Spring of Goliath) near Nazareth, they met their first great defeat.

The victory of 'Ayn Jālūt was largely due to the Egyptian general Baybars. From 1250 till 1517 Egypt and Syria were ruled by the Mamluk Sultans, members of a military caste who recruited their ranks from slaves of Turkish, and later Circassian origin. When Baybars became Sultan in 1261, he gave refuge in Cairo to the sole 'Abbāsid survivor of the massacre at Baghdad, and proclaimed him Caliph. Mamluk Egypt thus added a show of religious authority to its actual leadership of the Islamic world. Against the Crusaders Baybars began a series of determined campaigns which ended with their complete expulsion from the Holy Land after the fall of Acre in 1293. Baybars was himself a Turk from the Volga region, and in 1263 he concluded with Berke Khan, now a Moslem and leader of the Golden Horde, an alliance against the still unconverted Il-Khans of Persia. By thus playing on jealousy between rival Mongol rulers, Baybars ensured that the Il-Khans dare not exert their full strength in later attacks on his Syrian frontier.

But by the end of the thirteenth century the great crisis of Islam was over and its future secure. For when in 1295 Ghāzān Mahmūd usurped from his cousin the throne of the Il-Khans, his success was due to native Persian aid, and he thus found it expedient to re-establish Islam as the state religion. China and Persia had now both absorbed their nomad invaders, and in spite of all the preceding carnage and destruction one practical advantage of Mongol dominion over Asia remained; banditry had been suppressed, and under the *pax tatarica* the overland trade-routes between the Near and Far East were safer than ever before. This was the time of the first European journeys to the Far East. John of Pian del Carpine (1246) and William of Rubruck (1253–4) reached Mongolia; Niccolo and Maffeo Polo went twice to China itself, between 1260 and 1269 and again between 1271 and 1295, when they were accompanied by the young Marco Polo and entered the service of the Yüan Emperor Kubilai Khan. Persia re-

2

mained hostile to Egypt under Ghāzān Khan (1295–1304) and Uljaitu (1304–16), but happier relations developed with the exchange of embassies between the two countries under Abu Sa'īd (1316–35). A curious situation had arisen during the thirteenth century through the jealousy between the Il-Khan Mongols of Persia and their neighbours to the north, the Mongols of the Golden Horde in South Russia; Hulagu and Berke Khan actually went to war during the Polos' first visit to Sarai on the Volga in 1262. Unlike the Il-Khans, the Golden Horde had already been converted to Islam, and for a long time after their alliance with the Mamluks of Egypt in 1263 the Volga-Nile 'axis' maintained extraordinarily close religious and cultural ties. After Abu Sa'īd's death in 1335 the Il-Khan Mongol Empire in Persia rapidly dissolved into a number of petty principalities, which in time were swept away by the great Timur after 1380.[1] Nor did the Mongols survive much longer in China, where the native Ming dynasty overthrew the Yüan in 1368. But in both the Near and Far East there was no break in the new artistic developments that had begun under the rule of the barbarian invaders.

The formation of a 'Mongol' style

Apart from Hulagu's astronomical observatory at Marāgha, practically no important buildings were erected in Persia under the Mongols until the accession of Ghāzān Khan in 1295.[2] In the 'renaissance' of Persian art that followed, Ghāzān built a great tomb-mosque for himself at Tabrīz, and his Persian vizier Rashīd al-Dīn laid out a sumptuous new quarter, the Rab'-i-Rashīdī, where art and scholarship were vigorously pursued. Uljaitu (1304–16) founded a new capital at Sultānīya, where the impressive ruin of his tomb-mosque can still be seen. Among the minor arts, it is probable that the richly patterned silk textiles were the most characteristic works of the whole Mongol period. They formed the bulk of the diplomatic gifts exchanged between princes. According to Rashīd al-Dīn, Ghāzān Khan's embassy to the Yüan Emperor Timur in 1298 returned with a great array of silk brocades. The silk trade extended west into Europe; already in 1295 the inventory of the Holy See in Rome listed many *panni Tartarici*, decorated mainly with flowers, foliage and animals and birds in gold on a coloured ground.[3] The colour black is frequently mentioned, and a pattern *ad pineas* which might be a version of the Chinese lotus.

[1] See p. 32.
[2] See generally Donald N. Wilber, *The Architecture of Islamic Iran: The Il Khanid Period*, Princeton, 1955.
[3] E. Molinier, *Inventaire du Trésor du Saint-Siège sous Boniface* VIII (1295), Paris 1888, *passim*, especially nos. 804–994, 1143–72, 1263–81. No. 804 for *litteris tartaricis*; nos. 973, 974 for *panno de Taur.*...

'Tartar stuffs' was probably a generic name in Europe for all Islamic and Chinese work; a piece *cum litteris tartaricis* evidently had an Arabic inscription. Two pieces described as *de Taur . . .* must have been made at the Il-Khan capital, Tabrīz (Tauris). In the tombs of Pope Benedict XI at Perugia (1304), Cangrande I at Verona (1329), and Duke Rudolph IV of Austria (1365) were found contemporary oriental silks, the last inscribed with the name of the Il-Khan Abu Sa'īd; others have been preserved in church treasuries at Danzig and Regensburg. These silks show a strange mixture of Chinese and Islamic elements in design, and modern students of textiles seem unable to agree whether they were made in China, Turkestan, South Russia, Persia, or Egypt.[1] According to Abu'l-Fidā (an eye-witness), an embassy of 1323 from Abu Sa'īd the Il-Khan brought to Egypt a gift of seven hundred silks, presumably made in Persia, which had already woven into them the name and titles of the Mamluk Sultan al-Nāsir Nāsir al-dīn Muhammad ibn Qalāwūn (1293–1340), for whom they were designated.[2] It would be too much to hope that they included the two surviving silk patterns that bear the title al-Nāsir.[3] One of the vestments at Regensburg is inscribed 'made by the Master 'Abd al-'Azīz'. It and similar silks formerly at Danzig[4] are particularly relevant to our inquiry because of their style. The ornament is arranged in broad and narrow bands; there are inscriptions in the bold cursive Arabic script known as *thuluth*; and the bands themselves are subdivided into square or rectangular panels containing Chinese animals, lotus-palmettes, crescents, and small, neat diaper or trellis-patterns. Black outlining of the patterns contributes a peculiar note to

[1] Some have gilt applied flat on one side of fine leather threads. Pieces with this curious technique are commonly assigned to China, on the unsatisfactory grounds that flat-gilt paper threads were used in China at a much later date. None of the pieces came from China itself. It seems doubtful whether weavers in China would use Arabic inscriptions as ornament, even on pieces intended for export to the west. Arabs and Persians resident in China were merchants rather than craftsmen. The Arabic inscriptions on Chinese blue-and-white porcelain of the reign of Chêng Tê (1506–21) are no true parallel; these were made to special order for the Muslim eunuchs who dominated the Court in this particular reign. Good illustrations in *A Survey of Persian Art*, London and New York, 1938, Plates 996 ff. (text, vol. 3, pp. 2042 ff., very unreliable). For the Regensburg vestments, *Sakrale Gewänder des Mittelalters*, Ausstellung, München, Bayerisches Nationalmuseum, 1955, no. 60.

[2] *Abulfedae Annales Muslemici*, ed. Reiske and J. G. C. Adler, Hannover, 1794, vol. 5, p. 359.

[3] A. F. Kendrick, *Catalogue of Muhammadan Textiles of the Medieval Period*, Victoria and Albert Museum, London, 1924, nos. 957, 959. This and earlier books incorrectly state that his name also appears on the well-known parrot silk at Danzig.

[4] W. Mannowsky, *Kirchliche Gewänder und Stickereien aus dem Schatz der Marienkirche*, Danzig, 1929, vol. 1, no. 3; vol. 2, nos. 30–33. These silks are now shown in the Germanisches Museum at Nürnberg.

the colour-scheme. The 'stripe and panel' arrangement, no less than the motives themselves, is so characteristically Mongol that we shall not be surprised to find an essentially similar treatment of designs on pottery made during the fourteenth century in Persia, Syria, and Egypt. It would even seem that the potters were trying to produce a 'textile effect', with their chief motives shown light against a ground broken into a series of graduated darker tones. A similar 'textile effect' is apparent in much of the fourteenth-century blue-and-white porcelain made under the Mongol Yüan Emperors in China.

Though textiles were doubtless the chief medium through which Chinese designs reached the Near East, we should not discount the influence of Chinese paintings on silk or paper. Four albums in the Topkapu Serai Library at Istanbul contain an extraordinary medley of drawings, some definitely Chinese, some Persian, the rest in hybrid Mongol-Turkish-Chinese styles whose place of origin in Asia, or even South Russia, remains a subject for debate.[1] These albums were probably assembled in Eastern Persia during the first half of the fifteenth century, and preserve for us a fascinating conspectus of the loose sheets circulating in the Near East about that time. We could reasonably infer that isolated drawings, largely Chinese, were current also at the beginning of the fourteenth century, for they certainly left their mark on the few Persian illustrated volumes of that date that have survived. A Bestiary compiled for Ghāzān Khan at Marāgha shortly before 1300 contains some miniatures in an older Persian or Mesopotamian style, and others of animals and birds in landscape whose sketchy drawing in wash and Chinese ink could almost have been done by a Chinese artist.[2] But the first great masterpieces of this Il-Khan school are two fragmentary manuscripts of the *History of the World* written for Uljaitu by his famous vizier Rashīd al-Dīn; one dated 706 H/1307 A.D. in Edinburgh University Library, the other of 714 H/1314–5 A.D. belonging to the Royal Asiatic Society, London.[3] Their large illustrations reveal a style of extraordinary power and originality, not only in the figures, many of which wear Mongol dress, but also in the attempt to render the aerial perspective of landscape in

[1] See articles by Oktay Aslanapa, Max Loehr, and R. Ettinghausen, in *Ars Orientalis*, vol. 1, Ann Arbor, 1955, pp. 77–103; and M. Ş. Ipşiroğlu and S. Eyüboğlu, *Sur l'Album du Conquérant*, Istanbul Üniversitesi Edebiyat Fakültesi Yayinlari; M. Ş. Ipşiroğlu, *Painting and Culture of the Mongols*, London, 1967.

[2] C. Anet, 'The Manafi-i Heiwan,' *Burlington Magazine*, vol. 23, London, 1913, pp. 224–31. *A Survey of Persian art*, ed. A. U. Pope, London and New York, 1938, Plates 819A, 821.

[3] Illuminating accounts of these are given by E. de Lorey, 'L'école de Tabriz: l'Islam aux prises avec la Chine,' in *Revue des arts asiatiques*, vol. 9, Paris 1935, pp. 27–39; and Douglas Barrett, *Persian Painting of the Fourteenth Century*, London (Faber), 1952.

a sparse and angular idiom very close to the Chinese. In contrast with the gay palette of earlier and later Persian painting the colour-scheme is here dominated by sombre black outlines and grey washes of Chinese ink, with areas of shading in silver. Later Mongol manuscripts, notably the scattered pages of the great 'Demotte' Shāh Nāmah[1] painted about 1335–50, show how the Persian book-painters set about assimilating the bleak Far Eastern elements into a more sumptuous style of their own. The other arts took far longer to recover from the sober vision whose impact the Rashīd al-Dīn manuscripts reveal in all its initial harshness.

The transition to the 'Mongol' style in pottery

The sober Mongol taste evident in the textiles and manuscripts inspired a new manner also in pottery, which spread from Persia to Syria and Egypt and persisted throughout the fourteenth century.

But this was no sudden development; it was foreshadowed by the appearance, about 1300, of Mongol figures and Chinese designs on pottery whose colour-schemes and techniques continued a tradition that reached back for more than a century. We may here conveniently reconsider the Persian scene before the Mongols arrived.

The seventy odd years preceding the first Mongol invasion of 1219 had been a brilliant epoch for the Persian potters; inspired by the delicate white Ting and *ying ch'ing* (*ch'ing pai*) porcelains of the Sung dynasty imported from China, they developed for the body of their own wares a vitreous composition of ground quartz and white clay which, in point of whiteness and translucency, was not inferior to the Chinese. To vessels sensitively fashioned from this rather brittle material they added decoration, first by the Chinese method of carving and incising the unfired paste, but soon by the purely Near Eastern techniques of painting over or under the glaze. The finest wares were those painted in 'gold lustre' and the so-called *mīnā'ī* enamel colours with gilding; cheaper wares, often of excellent artistic quality, were painted in a limited range of colours under the glaze, and required only a single firing. It becomes increasingly evident that the finest wares were made in very few places, from which they were exported far and wide.[2] Of such centres, Rayy near Teheran succumbed to the

---

[1] Barrett, *op. cit.* Plate 6. *A Survey of Persian Art*, Plates 835–42. Complete references, Doris Brian, 'A reconstruction of the miniature cycle in the Demotte Shāh Nāmah,' *Ars Islamica*, vol. 6, Ann Arbor, 1939, pp. 97–112.

[2] Quantities of fine pottery in excellent preservation were discovered during the second World War at Gurgān, near the south-east corner of the Caspian Sea. It had apparently been packed in large jars and buried by the local retailers before their flight from the Mongols in 1220. It nearly all appears to have been imported from the factories at Rayy and Kāshān; several typical pieces bear the signatures of

Mongols in 1220 and Raqqa in Northern Mesopotamia in 1259. The more famous potteries of Kāshān survived the Mongol attack in 1224, and a series of dated vessels and tiles enable us to follow the swift development and gradual decline of the local lustre-ware throughout the period 1203–1339. On the whole the style is very conservative; the Chinese dragon, phoenix, lotus, and cloud-scroll begin to appear only after 1300, along with border-patterns of large *naskhi* inscriptions in relief. Earlier writers on Persian ceramics have presumed the emergence of a rival centre for lustre-ware somewhere in the neighbourhood of Sultānābād;[1] but for this there is no documentary evidence whatever. The supposed 'Sultānābād' lustre-wares are in fact the later products of Kāshān, as is proved by the name of that place on tiles of similar style bearing dates right up to 1339.

Chance has preserved in an Istanbul library two manuscript copies of a work on precious stones written at Tabrīz in 700 H/1301 A.D. by a native of Kāshān who came from a well-known family of potters.[2] Abu'l-Qāsim 'Abdallah ibn 'Alī, the author, has added a chapter on the techniques of pottery current in his time, particularly 'lustre' and a *lajvardina* (blue) ware that had superseded the by then obsolete 'seven-colour' wares (he must mean those painted in the polychrome *mīnā'ī* enamels). We can easily identify the *lajvardina* wares, with their deep blue glaze and simple patterns in red, white, and leaf-gold;[3] in shape and decoration they are clearly related to the lustre-wares also made at Kāshān. There is a curious and unexplained passage in a letter received in 1308 by the vizier Rashīd al-Dīn at Tabrīz; it describes various gifts being sent to him via Basra by 'Alā al-Dīn Muhammad Shah I, Sultan of Delhi (1295–1315). These included objects of 'china' (the word normally used of Chinese wares)—'*lajvard* dishes and drinking-bowls; royal bowls (i.e. large ones) with floral designs; big sherbet-bowls with "seven-colour" decoration; wine-ewers in *lajvard* ornamented with gold designs; and *lajvard*

Kāshān potters. Kilns were found at Gurgān, but the only certainly local product is a relatively coarse ware roughly painted in black under turquoise glaze. See M. Bahrami, *Gurgan faïences*, Cairo, 1949, a work whose conclusions are criticized by the present writer in *Oriental Art*, vol. 2, London, 1950, p. 164.

[1] See especially A. U. Pope in *A Survey of Persian Art*, vol. 2, London and New York, 1939, pp. 1631–8. This view was uncritically accepted by the present writer in *Early Islamic Pottery*, London, 1947, pp. 30, 39, 40, but corrected in subsequent reprintings.

[2] Edited with German translation by H. Ritter, J. Ruska, F. Sarre, R. Winderlich, 'Orientalische Steinbücher und persische Fayencetechnik' (*Deutsches Archäologisches Institut, Istanbuler Mitteilungen*, Heft 3, Istanbul, 1935).

[3] A. Lane, *Early Islamic Pottery*, London, 1947, p. 43, Plate 75. Ettinghausen mentions a star-tile of this class dated 715 H/1315 A.D.: *A Survey of Persian Art*, vol. 2, p. 1691, no. 160. Abu'l-Qāsim mentions potters at Tabrīz and Baghdad, besides Kāshān, but does not say whether they made fine wares.

saucers and flat dishes.'[1] No contemporary Chinese ware could answer this description, and we can only conclude that Persian *lajvardina* wares traded to India were being sent back to Persia as diplomatic gifts. The ware also reached Sarai in South Russia.[2] A significant general observation may be made about both the Kāshān lustre and the *lajvardina* wares of around 1300; they are more thickly potted than their equivalents of a century earlier, making no play with the translucency of the material; they are also less sensitive in shape. It would appear that the potters were no longer attempting to re-create the virtues of the delicate Chinese *ying ch'ing* and Ting-type white porcelains that had so interested them earlier. Apart from one rather rare class of Persian pottery made shortly before and after 1300,[3] whiteness was studiously toned down as the fourteenth century advanced. The potters were to become more interested in shades of grey.

As we have seen, the Persian painters and weavers of about 1300 were profoundly influenced by imported Chinese drawings and textiles, with which they may not previously have been familiar. One is tempted to ask whether unfamiliar types of Chinese pottery or porcelain could have exercised a similar influence on the Persian potters. The answer is, no. The great Chinese novelty of the Mongol period, porcelain painted in blue-and-white, had scarcely begun to develop; it had no influence whatever on the typical Mongol 'Sultānābād' wares of Persia in the first half of the fourteenth century. The Chinese wares that reached the Near East, for some time before and after 1300, were still varieties of white porcelain and celadon, with carved or moulded decoration; odd pieces of Tz'ŭ-chou painted ware and perhaps of primitive blue-and-white were too few to attract much attention. The white pieces were of the so-called *ch'ing pai* or *ying ch'ing* class, with a faintly blue glaze;[4] these were soon supplemented by the harder and heavier white porcelains of the *shu fu* type.[5] The celadons came from the Lung Ch'üan and other kilns in Chekiang Province. With their

---

[1] Quoted by A. U. Pope, *A Survey of Persian Art*, vol. 2, p. 1639. The volume of 53 letters written by or to Rashīd al-Dīn was bequeathed to Cambridge University Library by E. G. Browne, who describes it in his *A Literary History of Persia*, vol. 3, Cambridge, 1928, p. 85, no. 47.

[2] B. D. Grekov and A. Yu. Yakubovsky, *The Golden Horde and its decline* (in Russian), Moscow and Leningrad, 1950, Fig. 40 (*lajvard* bottle, illustrated upside down). Fig. 43 shows an imported Chinese bottle of painted Tz'ŭ-chou ware.

[3] A. Lane, *Early Islamic Pottery*, Plates 94–6.

[4] At Fustāt in Egypt and on East African sites have been found fragments of large petal-back *ch'ing pai* bowls, a robust type probably made specially for export. They are not represented among the pieces from China in Western collections. See Leigh Ashton, 'China and Egypt,' *Oriental Ceramic Society Transactions*, vol. 11, London, 1933–4, p. 68 and Plate 29, nos. 13, 14.

[5] E.g. Basil Gray, *Early Chinese Pottery and Porcelain*, London, 1953, Plate 95. Fragments of *shu fu* type from Fustāt are in the Victoria and Albert Museum.

white body and thick grey-green glaze, fragments of these celadons are likely to be found in abundance on any Near Eastern site of the later thirteenth or fourteenth century. Many of the pieces which are described in western collections as 'Sung' are more probably of four-teenth-century date. That was the time when the export of celadon to the Near East reached its height, and when the Near Eastern potters made their most determined efforts to imitate celadon in their own unsuitable materials. It is probably through a mere accident of selection by the commercial excavators that so few of these imitations have been recovered from Persia. The dish and bowl here illustrated (1) can be identified as of fourteenth-century date by their light weight and loose, granular body; later Persian pieces have a heavier and better-vitrified paste. Hemispherical bowls of this class often have large Arabic pseudo-inscriptions in relief outside the lip, like Persian bowls of the fourteenth century in other techniques. In Egypt, great quantities of locally made celadon imitations have been found at Fustāt, always in fragments. The bowls and dishes often follow a Chinese peculiarity in their construction; a circular hole was pierced in the centre, and covered, before the application of the glaze, with a thin circular wafer moulded in the form of a rosette. A similar device, intended to circumvent the risk of fire-cracks, was employed in the big Yüan celadon trumpet-mouthed vases;[1] these were thrown with no bottom, and a thin porcelain cup was inserted before glazing to take its place.

The Chinese motives painted on Persian lustre and other pottery of about 1300—dragons, phoenixes, lotuses, cloud-scrolls—could not in the nature of things have been taken from Chinese celadon or white porcelain; they must have been borrowed from another medium, almost certainly textiles. Nevertheless, the celadon vessels had an unmistakable influence on the Persian pottery shapes. At the beginning of the thirteenth century two bowl-shapes, both indigenous, were standard forms in all the Near Eastern factories. One had a wide cylindrical foot-ring and almost straight expanding sides;[2] the other had a splayed pedestal foot and sides whose straight expansion curved

[1] E.g. the Percival David Foundation vase dated 1327; Basil Gray, *Early Chinese Pottery and Porcelain*, London, 1953, Plate 94. For the numerous examples imported to Egypt, F. Fichtner, 'Chinesische Sung Celadone in Ägypten und ihre Nachbildungen in Fustat,' *Ostasiatische Zeitschrift*, vol. 6, 1930, p. 74. The large deep bowls with rosette centres, virtually unknown in European collections, are well represented in the Topkapu Serai collection in Istanbul; one from Ardebil is illustrated by J. A. Pope, *Chinese Porcelains from the Ardebil Shrine*, Washington, 1956, Plate 128.

[2] A. Lane, *Early Islamic Pottery*, Plate 92B.

(1) *Plate* 86.

boldly upwards and inwards before reaching a slightly outcurved lip.[1] By the end of the century both were obsolete, and the commonest bowl-shape was almost hemispherical, with a low narrow foot and radiating petal-patterns in relief or painted on the outside.[2] This is the typical form of the Lung Ch'üan celadon petal-back bowls.[3]

Persian Mongol pottery: the 'Sultānābād types'

We now come to the new types of painted pottery that most clearly reflect the Mongol taste. The fourteenth century could well be described as the age of 'blue-and-black'—or more strictly, 'blue-and-grey'. Before the century was out, a foretaste had already appeared of the succeeding fashion for 'blue-and-white' directly influenced by Chinese painted porcelain. We have no reliable evidence to locate the important Persian kiln-sites during this period. Tabrīz, the capital of Ghāzān Khan (1295–1304), is discounted as a potting centre by present opinion in Persia; Sultānīya, the capital of Uljaitu (1304–16), is shown by kiln-wasters to have produced only a coarse and inferior ware painted in black under turquoise glaze.[4] The new types were mainly found in the region of the modern city of Sultānābād (founded in 1808), on the road from Hamadān to Isfahan; they were particularly well represented in the Kelekian collection, exhibited on loan at the Victoria and Albert Museum between 1910 and 1952.[5] No confirmed kiln-sites were discovered, and the name 'Sultānābād type' is here adopted for convenience only, to cover at least three different groups of fourteenth-century pottery. Not one piece bears a date, but we can assume that all three groups reached their prime well before the collapse of the Il-Khan dynasty in 1335, and that the period of their decline may have prolonged itself into the fifteenth century.

The first two 'Sultānābād types' (1) are closely related and might even have been made in the same kilns. Their potting is thick and rather clumsy. The body is of coarsely-ground, loosely knit, and imperfectly vitrified material; it is not a pure white, having usually

[1] A. Lane, *Early Islamic Pottery*, Plates 86, 87B, 90B.

[2] A. Lane, *Early Islamic Pottery*, Plates 64A, 75A, 93, 96B.

[3] E. Zimmermann, *Altchinesische Porzellane im Alten Serai*, Berlin and Leipzig, 1930, Plate 9; *Celadon Wares*, Oriental Ceramic Society Exhibition, London, 1947, nos. 18, 20, 37, 39, etc.

[4] D. Talbot Rice, 'Some Wasters from Sultānīya' in *Burlington Magazine*, vol. 60, 1932, pp. 252–3. Examples are in the collection of Mr. Gerald Reitlinger.

[5] *The Dikran K. Kelekian Collection of Persian and Analogous Potteries*, Paris, 1910. See also Gerald Reitlinger, 'Sultanabad', in *Oriental Ceramic Society Transactions*, vol. 20, London, 1944–5, pp. 25–34.

(1) *Plates 1–4; Colour Plate A.*

A. Persian ('Sultānābād' type); first half of 14*th century. Diam.* 7 *in.*
Victoria and Albert Museum. (*pages* 10–12)

a slight pink or buff tinge under the glaze and grey discoloration on the exposed foot where dirt has been absorbed. The glaze is thick and glassy, running down to form greenish pools inside the vessel and tear-drops outside; it is apt to develop a fine crackle, and is especially subject to decay which may spread an opaque iridescent film over the entire surface. Some very new-looking pieces are perfectly genuine, having been discovered intact in an ancient store; on the other hand there exist modern forgeries of the second type which are far more dangerous than most of their kind. Among the shapes, the most characteristic is a bowl with an angular profile and a wide flat lip overhanging the interior (1), an exaggerated development of a form already known in the thirteenth century. Other bowls have straight or convex sides, tending towards a hemisphere; at the bottom they run to a point which appears on the reverse as a raised cone inside the foot-ring. There are dishes with narrow feet and flat rims (2), albarello-shaped jars (3), and fat jars with straight-sided necks tapering inwards. A small bowl with vertically-faceted sides has a spreading pedestal foot.

In the first type the painting is laid directly on the white body. Every detail is outlined in a soft greenish-black, which gives a pervading *grisaille* effect to the whole. A skilfully graded series of darker tones is built up by tiny dots (often in groups of three) on dresses and on animal figures; by curved black hatching in the background of the plant-motives; and by limited areas or backgrounds in solid dark blue. Some of the trefoil-shaped leaves are washed in with a thick pale blue slip and with a transparent turquoise, which has a peculiarly jewel-like effect. The general aim is to reduce to a minimum the white areas, which thus gain in luminosity against their softly shaded surroundings (4). The colour-scheme of the second type is even more original (5); the white ground disappears entirely under a coat of greenish or brownish grey slip, on which the highlights are applied in a thick white slip that stands up in perceptible relief; black is again used for all outlines and for background-hatching; the dark blue sometimes appears in spots on the white, but the turquoise is omitted altogether.

As may be seen from the illustrations, the painted designs are arranged in wide and narrow bands interrupted by medallions and wide or narrow rectangular panels—the same 'panel style' that we have mentioned as being so characteristic of certain Mongol textiles. Human figures are often recognizable as Mongols by their dresses:

---

(1) *Plate* 4; (2) *Plate* 2B; (3) *Plate* 3;
(4) *Plates* 2, 3; (5) *Colour Plate A, Plates* 1, 4.

long loose robes and curious hats, sometimes with a crest of owls' feathers. Rashīd al-Dīn describes how, in the bad old days before Ghāzān Khan, the Mongol falconers would go about wearing owls' feathers in their caps and belts, and belabour with their poles any natives they found wearing these insignia of privilege. On the pottery, as in the illustrated manuscript of Rashīd al-Dīn,[1] the Mongols are often shown conversing amiably with turbaned Persians; sitting out in the garden on folding camp-stools; or drinking some beverage that appears to be more palatable than their ancestral mares' milk. A bowl-fragment at Faenza[2] shows a prince enthroned, with two Mongol attendants, and his hunting cheetah lying chained at his feet. The background on these pieces is invariably filled with soft-looking large-leaved foliage, which gives a sylvan naturalism to the shy figures of animals and flying birds (1). As often as not the bird is a long-tailed Chinese phoenix, and even the naturalistic flying geese are taken from Far Eastern art. Before the spread of Mongol taste about 1300 birds in Near Eastern art never convincingly fly; at most they stand in profile with wings raised, or in the heraldic frontal stance with wings displayed. The stiffly stylized Chinese lotus-flower naturally has its place among the trefoil foliage on the 'Sultānābād' pottery. The white-ground bowls and dishes are almost invariably painted on the reverse with large spots in blue and smaller spots and dashes in black. On the outside of flanged bowls with the grey slip ground there is usually a band of large white pseudo-inscription at the shoulder, over a corona of petals that has been transformed into a ponderous arcade (2).

At their best, the 'Sultānābād types' of pottery are aesthetically as pleasing as any wares made earlier in the Near East. And despite the inclusion of Chinese motives in their painted designs, they are extraordinarily original. They have no close affinity with any ceramics of the Mongol period in China, though one might discover features in Chinese fourteenth-century wares that suggest the working of a similar taste. On Sung wares, designs were commonly carved in intaglio under the glaze; in the Yüan period designs on celadon and on the white *shu fu* wares tend to stand up from the surface in ever higher relief. It is perhaps fortuitous that the designs in raised white slip on the second 'Sultānābād type' sometimes look so like similar

[1] P. 5.
[2] 'Un cimelio della collezione Mereghi di Roma,' in *Faenza*, vol. 18, 1930, p. 68.

(1) *Plates 2, 4A, Colour Plate A.*
(2) *Plate 4B.*

designs on Chinese wares—the flying goose on a *shu fu* bowl,[1] the flying bird in a wreath shown in raised white slip on the dark blue ground of a spouted porcelain pouring-bowl in the Victoria and Albert Museum.[2] The hatched background of the 'Sultānābād' wares may be compared with a similar treatment on Chinese 'Tz'ŭ-chou' wares of the Mongol period, particularly those painted in black under a turquoise glaze.[3] Wares in the 'Sultānābād' manner were made during the fourteenth century in Syria and Egypt, but the Persian pieces are so superior in style as to leave no doubt where the fashion originated.

Standing somewhat apart from the first two Sultānābād types is a third (1), whose thinner potting and harder material show close affinities with the late Kāshān lustre-ware—a resemblance that extends to some of the designs.[4] In these wares, probably made at Kāshān, the white ground is left sufficiently exposed to dominate the colour-scheme. The patterns are crisply outlined in intense black; a vivid warm blue is used in broad interlacing bands, as well as for solid backgrounds; and limited areas are washed in with very pale transparent turquoise. Hemispherical bowls, flat-rimmed dishes, jugs and albarelli are the commonest shapes; more elaborate are the sixteen-lobed bowls (2). Figure-subjects, such as the Mongols in owls'-feather hats seen on Plate 6B, are rarely met with in this ware, and a certain poverty of ideas is shown in the monotonously repeated abstract patterns that conform so strictly to the panel convention. The bowls are almost invariably decorated with radiating wedge-shaped panels in which two or three motives recur in the same order—a *thuluth* inscription, blue interlacements, and plants reserved in a hatched ground. On the outside of the bowls are narrow petals outlined in blue.

Pottery of the Golden Horde in South Russia

We have already mentioned Sarai on the Volga, the capital of the Golden Horde. There were two cities of that name. Old Sarai was founded by Batu Khan before 1254, when William of Rubruck stayed there on his way from St. Louis of France to the Great Khan Mongka at Karakorum; its ruins lie near Selitrennoye, about seventy miles north up the river from the point near Astrakhan where it runs into the Caspian Sea. New Sarai, also called Sarai Berke, was apparently founded by Berke Khan (1257–66); it lies much further up the river

---

[1] John Ayers, 'Some wares of the Yüan dynasty,' *Oriental Ceramic Society Transactions*, vol. 29, 1954–5.

[2] J. Ayers, *loc. cit.*   [3] See p. 23.

[4] Compare the running fox in the border of Plate 6B with that on the lustre bowl, A. Lane, *Early Islamic Pottery*, London, 1947, Plate 64A.

---

(1) *Plate 6, Colour Plate B;* (2) *Plate 6B.*

near Tsarev, some forty miles east of Stalingrad. Under Usbek Khan (1312–40) it became the capital, and its thoroughly Islamic character was revealed by the excavations carried out in 1843–51 and again after the first World War. New Sarai was utterly destroyed by Timur when he overthrew Toktamish, leader of the Horde, in 1395, where-upon Old Sarai once more became the capital. These two cities in turn played a role of peculiar importance in the economic life of the Near East. One of the major routes of communication between Europe and China led via the Crimea, where the Genoese merchants had settle-ments, to Sarai; and south-eastwards from there to Urgenj, on the River Oxus where it runs north into the sea of Aral. We can see what Sarai meant to Persia from the surviving trade-accounts of a Shīrāz merchant. He started in 1438 from Shīrāz in South Persia with a caravan of Indian spices and other wares, and proceeded via Yezd, Herāt, and Urgenj to Sarai. There he sold his stock and bought raw and woven silk imported from China, and woollen cloth imported from Europe. He was able to sell this in Persia on his return in 1440 for more than four times the value of his original outlay.[1]

The finds at New Sarai, now in the Hermitage at Leningrad, have been described in several Russian publications difficult of access. They include unglazed and glazed pottery vessels, glazed tiles, and fully developed tile-mosaic resembling that in Timurid buildings at Samar-qand. From the discovery of kilns it appears that the tiles and most of the pottery were locally made. Most striking is a series of pottery bowls, painted in black outline and thick white slip on a grey ground, with spots of blue on the white patterns. One shows a goose in a central medallion (I); others have intersecting triangles and rosettes. These are surrounded by zones of comma-shaped white leaves or imitation Arabic inscriptions. The bowls are painted outside with white radiating petals.[2] This ware is closely related in style and date to that of our second 'Sultānābād type', from which it differs in the shape of the bowls and in the more stiffly conventional style of drawing. A pear-shaped bottle and various fragments[3] look remarkably like the

[1] Walther Hinz, 'Ein orientalisches Handelsunternehmen im 15 Jahrhundert,' *Welt des Orients*, Heft 4, Stuttgart, 1949.

[2] Three fragments in colour illustrated by F. V. Ballod, *Privolzhskie 'Pompei'* (The Volga-Pompeii), Moscow and Leningrad, 1923, Plate 25; three more bowls by B. D. Grekov and A. Yu. Yakubovsky, *Zolota orda i ee padeine* (The Golden Horde and its decline), Moscow and Leningrad, 1950, Figs. 35–7; one of these figured in the same authors' *La Horde d'Or* (French transl. F. Thuret), Paris, 1939, Plate 5.

[3] Bottle in Grekov and Yakubovsky, *op. cit.*, Paris, 1939, Plate 5; fragments (in colour) in Ballod, *op. cit.*, Plate 18.

(I) *Plate 5.*

THE FOURTEENTH-CENTURY MONGOL STYLE

Syrian-Egyptian wares in the blue-and-white 'panel style' shortly to be described, and it should be noted that the close alliance struck with Egypt under Berke Khan in 1263 was renewed under Usbek Khan (1312–40). Certain objects at New Sarai have been identified as Egyptian imports, among them an inscribed marble candlestick. There are also imported Chinese celadon and Tz'ŭ-chou wares; and a locally made square tile is painted with lotuses growing in water, a design which must have been taken from fourteenth-century blue-and-white porcelain.[1]

Syrian and Egyptian wares in Mongol style

Egypt escaped invasion by the Mongols, and Syria was never permanently occupied by them. After the fall of the Egyptian Fātimid dynasty in 1171 both countries were ruled by the Ayyūbids (1171–1250), and thereafter by the Mamluks (1250–1517). The fine series of Fātimid lustre-wares came to an end with the burning of the potters' quarter at Fustāt in 1169. Some of the potters may have moved to Syria, where a post-Fātimid lustre-ware of excellent quality came to light in the Danish excavations at Hamā.[2] Others perhaps went to Raqqa in Northern Mesopotamia, just beyond the Syrian border. The Raqqa kilns were very active till the city was destroyed by the Mongols in 1259, making a characteristic lustre-ware and cheaper varieties painted in blue, black and red under the glaze[3] (the latter are hard to distinguish from underglaze-painted wares made at the same time in Egypt). In contrast with the more softly rounded painting on contemporary Persian pottery of Rayy and Kāshān, the sketchy drawing on these Arab Ayyūbid wares has a sharp, nervous vitality; there are wiry prancing animals and birds, spiky foliage, and thin stems with tight little comma-shaped leaves.

It would be reasonable to suppose that in Egypt pottery was painted or carved in this Ayyūbid style throughout the thirteenth century. What happened in Syria after the fall of Raqqa remains obscure, but some potters conversant with the lustre technique probably escaped to Damascus. A fine large jar in a French private collection bears an inscription: 'This is one of the objects made for Asad al-Iskandarānī. Work of Yūsuf in Damascus';[4] it is painted in brassy lustre on a deep

[1] Grekov and Yakubovsky, *op. cit.*, 1950, Fig. 51.
[2] P. J. Riis and V. Poulsen, *Hama, Fouilles et Recherches 1931–1938*, IV, 2: *Les Verreries et Poteries Médiévales*, Copenhagen, 1957, pp. 136–141, 152–156. I now recognize as from this Syrian fabric the four bowls, A. Lane, *Early Islamic Pottery*, London, 1947, Plate 28B, and G. Migeon, *Manuel d'art musulman*, vol. 2, Paris, 1927, Figs. 334, 335, 336. The first and last of these are known to have been found in Syria.
[3] A. Lane, *Early Islamic Pottery*, London, 1947, Plates 57–60, 77–81.
[4] I owe thanks for this reading to M. Jean David-Weill and Dr. L. A. Mayer.

blue glaze with ornamental Kufic letters and foliage in Ayyūbid style (1). The same style and technique, with lustre ranging from silver through brassy yellow to a dull brown, is seen on a good many blue-glazed fragments found at Fustāt and in the potters' quarter outside the East Gate of Damascus.[1] About a dozen large blue jars and albarelli survive intact in European collections; they are obviously of the same origin, but their drawing has lost the Ayyūbid sharpness and become broad and slovenly (2). In fact their favourite motives of large flying birds amid foliage, long-tailed peacocks, and big *thuluth* inscriptions closely resemble those on the commoner blue-and-black Syrian wares of the fourteenth century. A fragmentary ogee bowl in the Victoria and Albert Museum, of a metallic shape peculiar to Syria, has inside a design of water-plants that can only have been copied from Chinese blue-and-white porcelain.[2] A few bowl- or dish-fragments from Fustāt are painted in lustre on a dull purple, instead of a blue ground; and a large jar in the Godman collection has an unstained, greenish glaze covered with brownish lustre, in which are oval reserved panels containing arabesques.[3] The potters' quarter at Damascus is supposed to have been burnt by Timur in 1401, and that probably brought the manufacture of lustre-ware to an end. Isolated fragments of a different type from Fustāt have been adduced as evidence that lustre-ware was also made in Egypt during the fourteenth century— perhaps as the short-lived venture of a single potter.[4] It is more significant that during the fourteenth century the ancient technique of lustre-painting was near extinction in the Near East, and after 1400 failed completely. Egyptian connoisseurs had to look to the west for supplies of this luxury. Already in the fourteenth century many pieces were imported from the factories at Malaga in southern Spain; in the fifteenth they were followed by a flood from the potteries at Manises near Valencia.[5]

[1] G. Migeon, 'Nouvelles découvertes sur la céramique de Damas,' in *Revue de l'art ancien et moderne*, vol. 44, 1923, p. 383.

[2] No. C. 1281–1921, from Fustāt. Compare the blue-and-white dish, Plate 13A.

[3] *The Godman collection of Oriental and Spanish pottery and glass*, London, 1901, Plate 3.

[4] Mohamed Mostafa, 'Two Fragments of Egyptian Lustre-painted Ceramics from the Mamlouk Period,' in *Bulletin de l'Institut d'Egypte*, vol. 31, 1949, pp. 377–82.

[5] E. Kühnel, 'Loza hispanoarabe excavada en oriente,' in *Al Andalus*, vol. 6, Madrid, 1942, pp. 253–68; a description of pieces in the Berlin Museum. Others from Fustāt are in the Victoria and Albert Museum. The Museum of Islamic Art, Cairo, has numerous fragments of fourteenth-century Malaga lustre pottery that have not yet been studied, including large vessels of the 'Alhambra' type.

(1) *Plate 7*; (2) *Plates 8, 9*.

More numerous are the fourteenth-century Syrian wares painted in blue and black (I). This class is well represented by a series of large vases and albarelli which share with the lustre-painted pieces the peculiar distinction of being almost the only pre-sixteenth-century Islamic pottery that has survived above ground since it was made. Most of the examples were discovered in Sicily, by nineteenth-century collectors who at first proposed for them the title 'Siculo-Arabian'. The vessels in fact appear to have served as containers for the exotic fruits and spices that were exported from Damascus to Europe and there retailed largely by the apothecaries. 'XI *pots de domas*' were listed among the possessions of a Valencian apothecary in 1329; and in 1364 Guillem Metge, apothecary of Barcelona, owned no less than 59 *pots de domas* of various sizes and 28 *escudelles* (bowls) *de domas*.[1] French and Italian inventories of the fourteenth and fifteenth centuries suggest that Damascus pots were treasured for their own sake, and even mounted in precious metal, after their contents of green ginger and the like had been consumed.[2] In 1420 a Moorish potter of Manises near Valencia contracted to make for a Milanese merchant 720 *pots* . . . *à la domasquina* . . . *dauratos et de çafre argentatos* to match a sample he had been given, probably a somewhat older Syrian jar;[3] and from that time onwards wares decorated *à la domasquina*, persumably in lustre on a blue ground, became one of the standard types made by Valencian potters. In Syria fragments of the blue-and-black class have been found on the site of the potters' quarter at Damascus, at Baalbek, and at Hamā;[4] but they are also very well represented at Fustāt, where

---

[1] M. Olivar Daydí, 'La vajilla de madera y la cerámica de uso en Valencia y en Cataluña durante el siglo XIV' (*Anejo número 2 de Anales del Centro de Cultura Valenciana*), 1950, pp. 22, 23, 27, 41.

[2] 1380, Charles V of France: no. 2202, un petit pot de terre, en façon de Damas: no. 2244, ung pot de terre à biberon, sans garnison, en la façon de Damas (J. Labarte, *Inventaire du mobilier de Charles V roi de France*, Paris, 1879). 1416, French Royal accounts, Hotel de la Royne: 'à Regnault Morel pour un pot de Damas plein de gingembre vert' (quoted by C. D. E. Fortnum, *A descriptive catalogue of the maiolica, etc., in the South Kensington Museum*, London, 1873, p. 9). 1420, Duke of Burgundy: no. 4201, 1 pot de terre, de l'ouvraige de Damas, blanc et bleu, garni le pié et couvercle qui est de jaspre d'argent doré à une ance d'un serpent d'argent doré (Comte de Laborde, *Les ducs de Bourgogne*, Paris, 1851, vol. 2, p. 258). 1456, Florence, Piero di Cosimo de' Medici: 3 alberegli domaschini e 3 scodelle di terra domaschina (E. Müntz, *Les collections des Médicis au XVe siècle*, Paris and London, 1888, pp. 25, 26).

[3] A. Van de Put, *Hispano-Moresque Ware of the Fifteenth Century: Supplementary Studies and Some Later Examples*, London, 1911, pp. 8, 15. *Idem, The Valencian Styles of Hispano-Moresque Pottery*, New York, 1938, p. 39.

[4] F. Sarre, *Keramik und andere Kleinfunde der islamischen Zeit von Baalbek*, Berlin and Leipzig, 1925. P. J. Riis and V. Poulsen, *op. cit.*, pp. 204–224.

(I) *Plates* 10–12.

almost impossible to distinguish between local Egyptian wares and those imported from Syria.

The potting of the Syrian 'blue-and-black' wares is heavy and robust, and their general finish is more careless than that of the contemporary Persian 'Sultānābād types' from which they evidently derived. The coarse material is whiter and harder than the Persian; the thick glassy glaze has a greenish tinge and sometimes develops a wide crackle. The blue is usually blackish, but occasionally bright and warm in tone; a transparent turquoise is sparingly used; and a few pieces have details in the thick brownish-red found on the earlier Ayyūbid pottery of Fustāt and Raqqa. Besides the typical large jars, albarelli, flat-rimmed dishes, and petal-backed bowls, a squat, ogee jar painted inside and under the flat foot (1) may be noted as a shape peculiar to Syria. It is found also in engraved and inlaid brass. The typical panel system of decoration is well shown in Plates 10 and 12; the medallions and leaf-shaped compartments are heavily outlined in blue, and the dots on the seeded grounds are arranged diamond-wise in groups of four. As on the contemporary Mamluk engraved metalwork, circular medallions containing heraldic devices are often incorporated among the designs. Quite a number of bowl-centres contain in a medallion the inscription 'made in the year forty-four', or 'the year forty-five'—the date 744 or 745 H/1343–4 A.D., omitting the hundreds; such pieces have turned up both at Hamā and at Fustāt, and provide a useful check for the general chronology of the Mongol style in pottery. The Syrian potters also painted some of their wares in a manner recalling the second 'Sultānābād type', with geese, peacocks, and running animals in a field of helplessly scattered trefoil-leaves (2). There is no prepared ground of grey slip, so that the raised slip-painting of the leaves and figures only shows slightly whiter than the greenish tone of the body seen through the glaze. Heavy blue lines on the figures do little to clarify their feeble drawing.

A somewhat similar, and hardly more successful attempt at animal-painting was made in Egypt, usually on the middle of dishes. Here no white slip was used; the walking animals or birds are shown walking among growing plants reserved against a background of solid blue. In the foreground there is sometimes a stylized pool with a fish in it—a motive familiar in the thirteenth-century Kāshān lustre-ware. But the Egyptian potters also made some surprisingly effective imitations of the 'Sultānābād' pottery bowls with a grey slip ground. They could easily be mistaken for the originals, were it not for the sparing addition of a colour not known at this time in Persia—a thick brown-red

_____

(1) *Plate* 12B; (2) *Plate* 11.

18

*B. Persian ('Sultānābād' type); first half of 14th century. Diam. 8 in.
The Keir Collection. (page 13)*

slip, used for the beaks and feet of the walking geese that form the favourite designs. Human figures are conspicuously absent from the decoration of fourteenth-century Syrian and Egyptian pottery, nor are they common on the engraved and inlaid Mamluk metalwork.

Another fourteenth-century type peculiar to Egypt is a variant of the blue-and-black 'panel' style, remarkable for its fine quality. The objects are all small bowls or flat-rimmed dishes, never more than about eight inches in diameter, and very thinly and sensitively shaped (1). The painting is of miniature-like delicacy, of close texture, drawn in very fine black lines. In the centre is usually a medallion containing a stylized blue-spotted plant reserved in a dark blue ground, from which radiate wedge-shaped panels containing stylized foliage, inscriptions, or a diaper of interlacing Y-shaped motives. The panels are separated by narrower bands of cross-hatching in blue; and very occasionally there are touches of brown-red or an opaque pale green. The low foot-ring is glazed inside and often inscribed in black with the name of a potter. In fact the Mamluk potters revived the practice of signing their wares that had been so common in Egypt during the Fātimid period. About thirty names have been recorded by scholars whose comments, largely fanciful, are not always easy to follow.[1] Some of the potters have foreign names—al-Hormuzī ('the man from Ormuz'), ash-Shāmī ('the man from Damascus') and so on; but it would be very rash to credit these individuals with the introduction to Egypt of styles that cannot be shown to have developed elsewhere. Egyptian pottery underwent considerable changes of style from the fourteenth to the fifteenth century, particularly when Chinese blue-and-white porcelain imposed a new fashion. Theoretically the signatures of potters should help us to recognize the stages reached during each working lifetime. But unfortunately we cannot be sure that the 'signature' is that of an individual rather than the mark of a workshop that operated through successive generations. The commonest signature, that of Ghaibī (who also calls himself Ghaibī ash-Shāmī and Ghaibī at-Tawrīzī ('the man of Tabrīz'), is commonest on blue-and-white pieces, some of them imitating Chinese types that can hardly be dated earlier than the reign of the Emperor Hsüan Tê (1426–35); but it also occurs on the miniature blue-and-black radial bowls which we should be inclined to date in the middle of the fourteenth century. And as for the theory that new styles in Egypt can only have been

---

[1] D. Fouquet, *Contribution à l'étude de la céramique orientale*, Cairo, 1900. Aly Bey Bahgat and F. Massoul, *La céramique musulmane de l'Egypte*, Cairo, 1930. A. Abel, *Gaibi et les grands faïenciers égyptiens d'époque mamlouke*, Cairo, 1930.

(1) *Plate* 16B, *left upper and lower.*

introduced by potters from Syria or Persia, it is enough to say that by far the commonest 'signature' on the miniature bowls is that of al-Ustādh al-Misrī, 'the Egyptian Master'. The tantalizing problem of the signatures is merely an incident in the long-drawn-out tragedy of Fustāt, where nine centuries of medieval Egyptian pottery are known to us through fragments undimmed by time or weather, and less than a dozen vessels have survived complete.

2

FIFTEENTH-CENTURY
BLUE-AND-WHITE

The new blue-and-white style in China

The Chinese porcelains and stoneware that were imported to the Near East continuously from the beginning of the ninth century were always considered more valuable than the native wares, and early Arab writers leave us in no doubt as to the qualities for which they were particularly admired. First, the intense, resonant hardness of their material; then the whiteness of the porcelain, and its translucency. Al-Bīrūnī and ath-Thaʻālibī, both writing in the first half of the eleventh century, named in order of preference the 'apricot-coloured' ware (celadon); the 'cream-coloured' (white porcelain); and the 'mottled' (stoneware streaked with colour in the glaze). The last-named may have been a retrospective reference to certain wares of the T'ang dynasty (618–906). Under the Sung (960–1279) the bulk of the imports were celadon and white porcelains: wares whose serene beauty was inherent in their materials, a dense and hard body perfectly united with a rich but sober-toned glaze. For added decoration they had only the most reticent carved and incised designs.

The debt of the Islamic potters to the Chinese is sufficiently indicated by the fact that they habitually gave the name *sini* ('china') to the wares of fine artistic quality which they made themselves. Twice only did they seriously attempt to capture the rare quality of porcelain —in ninth-century Mesopotamia, by applying an opaque white glaze to vessels of soft buff earthenware, and in twelfth-century Persia, where they adopted for all their fine wares a translucent material white throughout its substance. But on both occasions the low-fired Near Eastern clays proved inadequate to sustain the illusion, and the potters passed on to discover the field where their own true genius lay —in painted decoration, richly coloured, whose various techniques were still unknown, and indeed unsought, in the Far East. Even in their monochrome wares, initially inspired by the sober grey-green

21

celadon, they showed a congenital preference for brighter tones of turquoise, purple, and blue.

For five centuries, then, the paths pursued by the Chinese and Islamic potters had diverged, with only occasional points of contact. What we have now to consider is a radical change of direction on the part of the Chinese, who were converted to the cause of painted decoration, and thenceforward trod the path that had so long been followed in the Near East. The causes, and the stages, of their conversion have hitherto been little explored;[1] but there is strong reason to believe that it took place under the Mongol Yüan Emperors (1280–1368), partly owing to influences from the Near East which reached China at a time when political changes had made that country particularly receptive to foreign ideas. It is now certain beyond reasonable doubt that the cobalt-ore for painting the earliest Chinese blue-and-white porcelain was imported from Persia; and it is fair to assume that the method of using it was suggested by actual examples of Persian or other Islamic pottery. This would be the single potters' technique of major importance which China learned from the Near East.

The symptoms of change affect all the very diverse types of ceramics made in China during the Yüan period, even the monochrome celadon which had so perfectly embodied the Sung ideal. On certain pieces of celadon an attempt is made to modify the monochrome in favour of a two-colour effect; the glaze is dappled here and there with the large iron-brown spots called *tobi seiji* by Japanese collectors; or fish, rosettes and the like, moulded in low relief, are left unglazed and coloured with a wash of orange red (from iron) which contrasts strongly with the surrounding areas of grey-green. There is a tendency to bring up the carved designs, on both celadon and white wares, into even more salient relief—sometimes they are carved separately before being applied to the surface. A general coarsening of shapes, by Sung standards, appears quite deliberate; the suave contours break into sharply articulated members, with an effect more appropriate to metalwork—perhaps metalwork of foreign origin. It is significant that several new shapes in early Ming blue-and-white porcelain were directly imitated from imported Near Eastern vessels of inlaid and engraved brass.[2] One such metallic shape, found in fourteenth-century celadon, ch'ing pai (*ying ch'ing*), and porcelain painted in underglaze blue or red, may be of specifically Mongol

[1] New ground in this direction has been broken by John Ayers in his excellent paper, 'Some wares of the Yüan dynasty', published in *Oriental Ceramic Society Transactions*, vol. 29, 1954–5.

[2] Basil Gray, 'The influence of Near Eastern metalwork on Chinese ceramics,' *Oriental Ceramic Society Transactions*, vol. 18, London, 1940–1, pp. 47–60.

origin. It is a small, shallow, rimless and footless bowl, with a square open spout for pouring at the side;[1] under the spout there is often a loop for a string which would conveniently suspend the bowl from the person or from the saddle. These bowls would be used for ladling off into cups the contents (mares' milk?) of a larger open vessel. There is another type of shallow bowl which was obviously intended for the same purpose, and is about the same size. Instead of a spout, it has a dragon's-head handle at the side, again with a loop for suspension. These dragon-handle bowls are only known in silver. Their decoration combines Chinese and Islamic characteristics; one bears an added date 615 H/1220-1 A.D.; and all have been found in Siberia and South Russia, territory later occupied by the Mongols of the Golden Horde.[2]

The tendencies noted in the Yüan monochrome wares are naturally far more explicit in those with painted decoration—both the Tz'ŭ-chou stonewares and the new blue-and-white porcelain. The grey or buff stonewares made at Tz'ŭ-chou and other places in the north Chinese provinces of Chihli and Honan were unique among Sung pottery in having bold and expressive designs painted on their creamy-white ground. To the sophisticated taste of the Sung court they doubt-less appeared provincial, and they are not much appreciated in China even today. Yet they curiously foreshadow the revolution in favour of painted decoration. Even painting in green, red, and yellow over-glaze enamels, the natural alternative to blue-and-white in the later Ming porcelain, is shown by a dated specimen to have been practised by the Tz'ŭ-chou potters as early as 1201.[3] It is important to remem-ber that the Mongols were in possession of North China long before their final conquest of the Sung in the south; Kubilai Khan moved his capital to Peking in 1260. We should thus expect Near Eastern in-fluences to penetrate here first, by the land-routes across Asia. Such influence indeed appears in a small group of Tz'ŭ-chou wares, mainly smallish vases of *mei p'ing* shape, with fine linear brush-painting in black on a white slip under a clear turquoise glaze.[4] This colour-

[1] See Ayers *op. cit.* Jean Gordon Lee, 'Some Pre-Ming "Blue-and-White",' *Archives of the Chinese Art Society of America*, vol. 6, 1952, p. 37, Plate 3 (two blue-and-white pieces).

[2] P. W. Meister, 'Edelmetallarbeiten der Mongolen-Zeit', *Ostasiatische Zeitschrift*, N.F., vol. 14, 1938, pp. 209-13.

[3] Seiichi Okuda, *Masterpieces of Pottery and Porcelain in Japan*, vol. 2, Tokyo, c. 1933, Plate 75. For the type, W. B. Honey, *The Ceramic Art of China, etc.*, London, 1945, Plate 74A; Basil Gray, *Early Chinese Pottery and Porcelain*, London, 1953, p. 25, Plate 68. Gray's suggestion (*op. cit.*, p. 24) that the Tz'ŭ-chou potters derived their vastly superior *sgraffiato* technique from Near-Eastern pottery would not bear scrutiny in the light of the wares themselves; and his misleading description of the technique calls for the same kind of correction.

[4] Honey, *op. cit.*, Plate 75A; Gray, *op. cit.*, Plate 59 and pp. 24-5. Gray notes that such wares have been found in Korea and Manchuria in archaeological con-

scheme has no previous history in China,[1] but had been popular among
Near Eastern potters since the twelfth century. It is the colouring of a
common class of Persian wares made towards the end of the thirteenth century,[2] examples of which could have reached North China
at that time.[3] In shape and decoration the Tz'ŭ-chou black-and-
turquoise vases are so like early blue-and-white porcelain as to leave
no doubt of their dating in the fourteenth and early fifteenth centuries. The coiled foliage with which they are often painted is
reserved in a background of fine hatched lines, this creating the same
kind of 'textile effect' as we have noted in the Persian 'Sultānābād'
wares.

If imported Persian vessels account for the development of black-
and-turquoise painting at the Tz'ŭ-chou factories, the fact was of no
lasting significance. But blue-and-white is a different matter. It has
long been recognized that in China this technique has the character of
an alien importation. There is excellent painting in blue on Mesopotamian wares of the ninth century,[4] which long antedates any
similar manifestation in China—though here the painting is laid over
an opaque white glaze in its raw state, and not *under* a transparent
glaze.[5] Blue under the glaze was first effectively used from about 1200,
in wares made at Kāshān, Raqqa and Cairo;[6] it was apt to run in the
glaze, and for that reason throughout the thirteenth century it was
mainly applied as a wash to fill in patterns outlined in underglaze
black. At Kāshān and Raqqa the manufacture of these 'blue with black
outline' wares apparently ceased after the Mongol attacks of 1224 and
1259, and among later thirteenth-century Islamic wares in which the
colour is used, none is of particular distinction. We must presume that
the method of using the blue was suggested to the Chinese potters by
actual examples of Islamic pottery which reached China, though the
designs on these pieces may not have been sufficiently interesting to

texts that suggest a date earlier than the fourteenth century. As so often in the
Far East, 'archaeology' here conflicts with common-sense judgment based on style,
and must be treated with caution.
 [1] It is to be distinguished from the emerald-green glaze sometimes seen on Tz'ŭ-
chou wares, over black painting in a much broader and more characteristically
Sung style; cf. R. L. Hobson, *Catalogue of the George Eumorfopoulos Collection*,
London, 1925–8, vol. 3, no. C329, colour-plate.
 [2] Arthur Lane, *Early Islamic Pottery*, London, 1947, Plates 92A, 93.
 [3] A typical jar of this class, but with a colourless glaze, is illustrated by Seiichi
Okuda, *Masterpieces of Pottery and Porcelain in Japan*, vol. 2, Tokyo, c. 1933,
Plate 58. But it was taken to Japan in modern times.
 [4] Lane, *op. cit.*, Plates 8, 9.
 [5] Some contemporary T'ang 'three colour' wares have a glaze stained or dappled
with blue. Recent scientific analysis suggests that this blue may have been derived
from a cobalt-ore imported from Persia.
 [6] Lane, *op. cit.*, Plates 78, 79, 84–7.

be imitated. As for the cobalt-ore itself, the earliest Chinese written sources available suggest that it was first imported from the Near East. This is confirmed by recent scientific inquiry, which shows that the blue on porcelain painted in fourteenth-century style must have been derived from the high-grade Persian ore and not from the very different native ores of China.[1] In view of the indication supplied by the black-and-turquoise Tz'ŭ-chou wares, we would have expected to find the first attempts to use the related underglaze blue technique on wares made in North China. But in fact there is no considerable body of Tz'ŭ-chou wares painted in blue; at most, a few isolated examples suggest that the attempt was made and immediately failed. One of these examples is a jar in the British Museum, painted in dull grey-blue on a white ground with simple bands and an inscribed date equivalent to 1279.[2] It thus appears that the makers of the first blue-and-white Chinese porcelain did not acquire the technique through the mediation of the northern Tz'ŭ-chou wares;[3] they must themselves have seen Near Eastern pottery. And as the porcelain-factories were concentrated in and round Ching-tê Chên in the southern province of Kiangsi, their contact with the Near East would most naturally have been made via the south Chinese seaports to Canton and Chü'an Chou. We scarcely need the reminder of Marco Polo, himself a trusted official of Kubilai Khan for seventeen years, that wherever they went the Mongols preferred to rule through cosmopolitan advisers and showed particular favour to alien minorities. The colonies of Arab merchants at Canton and Chü'an Chou (which they called Zaitun) throve and increased. For them in the first place were imported those vessels of thirteenth- and fourteenth-century Syrian and Egyptian enamelled glass,[4] of engraved and inlaid brass, and presumably of Islamic pottery, which found their way to Ching-tê Chên and were seen by the makers of porcelain. By the middle of the fourteenth century Canton and Chü'an Chou were full of porcelain awaiting export in the reverse direction. Ibn Battūta, who visited them

[1] Sir Harry Garner, 'The Use of Imported Cobalt in Chinese Blue and White,' *Oriental Art*, N.S., vol. 2, 1956, pp. 48–50. Stuart Young, 'An Analysis of Chinese Blue-and-White,' *loc. cit.*, pp. 43–7.

[2] Soame Jenyns mentions another, *Ming Pottery and Porcelain*, London, 1954, p. 26; a pillow whose glaze is so badly decayed that the patterns painted in greyish blue can no longer be read.

[3] Brown-painted wares of Tz'ŭ-chou type were also made in South China at Yung Ho, in the same province of Kiangsi as the porcelain-kilns of Ching-tê Chên. But the painting on these would appear to have been influenced by that on the blue-and-white porcelain rather than the reverse. See A. D. Brankston, 'An Excursion to Ching-tê Chên,' *Oriental Ceramic Society Transactions*, vol. 16, London, 1938–9, p. 30, Plates 5, 6.

[4] C. J. Lamm, *Mittelalterliche Gläser und Steinschnittarbeiten aus dem nahen Osten*, Berlin, 1930, pp. 21–2, 255, 259, 262–3, etc.

about 1345, was thus incorrectly persuaded that porcelain was made there and nowhere else in China.[1] The bulk of what he saw was probably celadon and white ware, but much of the latter must already have been painted with decoration in blue, and a few pieces with decoration in underglaze copper-red. For this colour was used at least as early as the blue, but proved much less reliable. It is an interesting possibility that the potters may have seen Persian lustre-ware, and have been led to experiment with copper through hearing that this was the essential metal through which their exotic effect was obtained.[2]

It now seems barren to speculate on early blue-and-white made before the Yüan period, or outside the region of Ching-tê Chên,[3] where its evolution is suggested by fragments found on local kiln-sites. The body of the most primitive pieces is like that of the so-called *ch'ing pai* (*ying ch'ing*) porcelain, of rather brittle, loosely-knit structure, with a faintly bluish glaze. Other presumably early pieces have the more compact and massive body of the white wares with the moulded characters *shu fu* ('privy council'), the wares which a Chinese written source of 1387 describes as made for the Yüan court. The only secure landmark for dating is the very elaborately shaped and painted pair of altar-vases in the Percival David Foundation, which was made in 1351 for a shrine near Ching-tê Chên.[4] Comparison of style and technique help to distinguish earlier and more primitive pieces, and the later ones that bridge the gap till the reign of Hsüan Tê (1426–35), when it first became common practice to paint the reign-mark on good blue-and-white pieces. To judge from finds outside China, export of blue-and-white began when the ware was still in its most primitive stage,[5] and no distinction in quality was observed in pieces destined for the home and export markets. In fact it seems that Yüan court taste long remained apathetic, or even adverse, to the new painted wares. 'Official' orders in the fourteenth century appear to have been for the

---

[1] P. Kahle, 'Chinese Porcelain in the Lands of Islam,' *Oriental Ceramic Society Transactions*, vol. 18, 1940–1, pp. 37–8.

[2] But it is also possible that the use of underglaze copper-red was introduced to China from Korea, where it appears in decoration on celadon wares which may be of thirteenth-century date.

[3] The bones and confused tracks of his predecessors were reported by the last to perish in this desert, Soame Jenyns, *Ming Pottery and Porcelain*, London, 1953, Chapters 3 and 4. For safer guidance to the origins of blue-and-white, see Sir Harry Garner, *Oriental Blue-and-White*, London, 1954, Chapters 2 and 3; and John A. Pope, *Chinese Porcelains from the Ardebil Shrine*, Washington, 1956, pp. 38–45. (The last was received after my own text was finished.)

[4] Garner, *op. cit.*, Plate 6; often illustrated elsewhere.

[5] Very primitive bottles painted in underglaze blue and red were found at Gedi and Kilepwa in Kenya; J. S. Kirkman, *The Arab City of Gedi*, Oxford, 1954, pp. 13, 129, fig. 32D.

shu fu wares, which are white. The first Ming porcelains to bear an Emperor's reign-mark, and which were thus presumably made for the court, have the name of Yung Lo (1403–24) inscribed in archaic characters; these too are white, or much more rarely in underglaze red monochrome. They are of extraordinarily thin and delicate construction, and have almost invisible slip-painted or incised designs. In fact they seem to look back to the delicate Ting wares of the Sung dynasty in a deliberately conservative taste, as if they were ordered for the Emperor by Chinese officials of the old school. It seems possible that neither of the first two great Emperors of the Ming (Hung Wu, 1368–98: Yung Lo, 1403–23) had much personal interest in porcelain. Yung Lo himself was no conservative, but a ruler of wide vision, with foreign advisers; he repeatedly sent his fleet to display the might of China in the South Seas, and encouraged diplomatic exchanges with foreign powers. In 1419 an embassy from 'Dai Ming', Emperor of China, reached the court of Shāh Rukh of Persia at Herāt, bringing gifts of a falcon, various silks, and vessels of porcelain. Between 1419–1422 a return embassy, over 500 strong, was sent overland to China by Shāh Rukh and his kinsmen; it was accompanied by the painter Ghiyāth al-Dīn, who had instructions to make a careful record of what he saw by the way.[1] At two feasts given to the ambassadors as they approached the Chinese frontier at Su Chou he duly noted the porcelain plates, the jugs, bottles and large and small vases; but porcelain is not once mentioned in his fascinating description of the new palace at Peking, and of the many alarming encounters with Yung Lo himself, whose Muslim Counsellor Mawlānā Hājjī Yūsuf the Qādī instructed the visiting party on court etiquette. Persian horses and hunting-cheetahs were the gifts that most appealed to the testy old Emperor, who seems personally to have supervised the choice of presents for the ambassadors; falcons, silks of various kinds, and silver, but no porcelain. Perhaps the builder of the Forbidden City and the Porcelain Tower at Nanking thought table-ware beneath his notice. Certainly neither he nor any of his immediate predecessors is likely to have fostered a superior type of blue-and-white porcelain whose export was forbidden. The first certainly 'Imperial' blue-and-white is that bearing the reign-mark of Hsüan Tê. Earlier pieces, even if found outside China, may have been the very best made at their time.

The most considerable existing body of Chinese blue-and-white

---

[1] His account, a model of keen observation and accuracy, was incorporated in a contemporary history by 'Abd er-Razzāg: French translation by E. Quatremère, 'Notice de l'ouvrage persan qui a pour titre Matla-assaadeïn ou Madjma-albah-reïn,' in *Notices et extraits des manuscrits de la Bibliothèque du roi*, vol. 14, Paris, 1843, pp. 387–426.

porcelain datable in the fourteenth century is preserved in two great Near Eastern collections—that of the Ottoman Sultans in the Topkapu Serai at Istanbul;[1] and that deposited by Shāh 'Abbās I of Persia in the shrine of Sheikh Safī at Ardebil in 1611.[2] In both the pieces are robustly potted vases, bottles and dishes of considerable size. No doubt there were once many smaller pieces, but only at Ardebil have some of these survived the wear and tear of use. In view of what has been said in the last paragraph, the quality of these pieces must be the finest that could be produced at that time. At Istanbul the blue-and-white is shown alongside the contemporary carved celadon, with which it shows a remarkable affinity both in shapes and in motives of decoration. The Istanbul palace inventories suggest that in the fifteenth century the Ottoman Sultans as yet possessed little Chinese porcelain—5 pieces in 1495, 11 in 1501, 21 in 1505. By 1514 the total had risen to 83, no doubt swollen by loot from Tabrīz, which Selim I captured in his Persian campaign of that year. Unfortunately there follows a gap in the inventories, but there must have been great quantities of porcelain among the spoil brought back from the conquest of Syria and Egypt in 1516–17.[3] The collection from Ardebīl is smaller than that at Istanbul, but includes some thirty fourteenth-century pieces that must have been in Persia for over two hundred years before their presentation to the mosque in 1611.

The painting on the great fourteenth-century Chinese dishes at Istanbul and Ardebīl is carried out with such breadth and power that the more refined fifteenth-century pieces seem a little tame in comparison. The organization of their designs is often very complex, and it is not surprising that the Islamic potters took some time to master the strange new idiom. In making their imitations they at first tended to select certain details or self-contained designs that were easily understood. They had moreover to adapt their technique. As we have observed, the thirteenth-century Islamic potters had outlined their blue designs in black. The Chinese, in taking over the blue, had perforce to omit the black, which would not have withstood the extremely high temperature of the porcelain-kiln; they therefore painted their outlines in darker shades of blue. When eventually the

[1] E. Zimmermann, 'Altchinesische Porzellane im Alten Serai,' *Meisterwerke der Türkischen Museen zu Konstantinopel*, vol. 2, Berlin and Leipzig, 1930 (dating unreliable). J. A. Pope, 'Fourteenth-Century Blue-and-White: A Group of Chinese Porcelains in the Topkapu Sarayi Müzesi, Istanbul'. *Freer Gallery of Art Occasional Papers*, vol. 2, no. 1, Washington, 1952.

[2] F. Sarre, *Denkmäler persischer Baukunst*, Berlin, 1901–10, pp. 41–4, Plate 52. J. A. Pope, *Chinese Porcelains from the Ardebil Shrine*, Washington, 1956 (received after these pages were written).

[3] P. Kahle, quoting from an early seventeenth-century account, in *Oriental Ceramic Society Transactions*, vol. 18, London, 1940–1, pp. 41–2.

pure blue-and-white palette appears in the Near East, it can be recognized as a Chinese-inspired fashion by the style of the designs with which it is associated. We now have to consider these Near Eastern imitations and adaptations so far as they are available, bearing in mind that one question in particular calls for an answer. At what point of time did the new blue-and-white porcelains begin reaching the Near East in sufficient quantity to upset the traditional allegiance to celadon? If they can be dated by archaeological or other means, the earliest Islamic blue-and-white wares may help to tell us. There are indications that all over the Near East blue-and-white was being made before (but not long before) the end of the fourteenth century. In the fifteenth century it became the dominant fashion, though earlier styles persisted in a decaying form.

Syria

The most coherent evidence for the adoption of blue-and-white comes from Syria. Perhaps the most frequently-recurring design on fourteenth-century Chinese porcelain was a symmetrical arrangement of lotuses growing in water with swimming ducks in the foreground;[1] the spiky petals of the flowers were in outline filled with solid blue near the tips. An isolated flower closely resembling this, including the blue tips, is common on the fourteenth-century blue-and-black Damascus pottery with birds among foliage, described in the previous chapter.[2] The material found in the Danish excavations on the citadel hill at Hamā is all to be dated before the city was sacked by Timur in 1401, and among it was the Syrian blue-and-white dish shown in Plate 13A.[3] The garbled wave-and-rock pattern on the rim, and the lotus-scroll round the well, with its peculiar long leaves, are closely imitated from a fourteenth-century Chinese dish.[4] In the centre is a water-lotus bound by a ribbon, another fourteenth-century design which takes a more sophisticated form on pieces of the fifteenth century.[5] From Hamā too came a large Syrian blue-and-white bowl in

[1] John A. Pope, *Fourteenth-century Blue-and-White, Istanbul* etc., Plates 4, 5, 20, 27; *Ardebil*, etc., Plates 7, 8. Sir Harry Garner, *Oriental Blue and White*, Plates 5, 9B.

[2] P. 18.

[3] P. J. Riis and V. Poulsen, *op. cit.*, p. 224, fig. 777 and p. 226. The significance of this piece for dating the Chinese wares from which it was copied was pointed out by Vagn Poulsen in a letter to the *Burlington Magazine*, vol. 90, London, 1948, p. 50.

[4] Pope, *Istanbul* etc., p. 48, Plates B2, A5. Garner, *op. cit.*, Plates 8B, 11.

[5] Jean Gordon Lee, 'Some pre-Ming blue-and-white,' *Archives of the Chinese Art Society of America*, vol. 6, 1952, p. 37, Plate 3b, e (fourteenth century). Garner, *op. cit.*, Plate 13 (fifteenth century). Pope, *Ardebil*, Plates 30, 31 (fifteenth century).

the National Museum, Copenhagen, with typically Chinese floral designs and on the outside a zone of Chinese 'lotus panels' or 'false gadroons'.[1] The intact jar in Plate 14, which was found in Sicily, is of typically Damascus shape apart from the faceted sides enclosing vertical painted panels; these were evidently suggested by a Chinese vase of a type represented at Istanbul.[2] The stems with tendrils, short leaves, and oval chrysanthemums closely follow Chinese originals that are believed to date from about 1400.[3] The motives on the albarello, Plate 15, are rather carelessly drawn, but all have parallels on Chinese fourteenth-century porcelain except for the black-outlined heraldic shield of European shape. Professor L. A. Mayer informs me that the fleur-de-lis in this form is not a Mamluk device; it almost certainly represents the *giglio* of the city of Florence, and it is tempting to recall that in 1456 Piero di Cosimo de'Medici owned 3 *alberegli domaschini* which he may have received as a diplomatic gift.[4] Motives freely adapted from porcelain were also used in Syria on hexagonal blue-and-white wall-tiles, some of which are still *in situ* in the Türbe of at-Tawrīzī at Damascus, built in A.D. 1423.[5] Others from Damascus are in the Victoria and Albert Museum (1). A design of narrow-leaved waterweeds in clusters, found on some Chinese fourteenth-century pieces, suggested to the Syrian potters a very free and wild plant decoration which is usually painted in black alone or in black under a turquoise glaze.[6] It appears that the fourteenth-century 'panel style' persisted in Syria during the fifteenth century alongside wares painted in the new Chinese fashion. The simplified geometric patterns and *thuluth* inscriptions are coarsely painted in black and turquoise, blue now being omitted from the colour-scheme (2).

[1] Compare Pope, *Istanbul*, p. 48, Plate C5, C6; and Plate 24, the Hamā bowl is in his *Ardebil*, Plate 132, with other pieces. Compare also P. J. Riis and V. Poulsen, *op. cit.*, p. 226 and fig. 787.

[2] Pope, *op. cit.*, Plate 27; Garner, *op. cit.*, Plate 18.

[3] Jean Gordon Lee, 'An Exhibition of Blue-decorated Porcelain of the Ming Dynasty,' *Philadelphia Museum Bulletin*, vol. 44, no. 223, 1949, nos. 14, 15, 17. Soame Jenyns, *Ming Pottery and Porcelain*, London, 1954, Plate 19.

[4] See p. 17, n. 2. Piero's son, Lorenzo the Magnificent, received in 1487 a gift of Chinese porcelain sent from Egypt (letter from Pietro Bibbiena to Clarice de'Medici, quoted by A. Fabroni, *Laurentii Medicis Magnifici Vita*, Pisa, 1784, p. 337).

[5] See Rudolf M. Riefstahl, 'Early Turkish tile-revetments in Edirne,' in *Ars Islamica*, vol. 4, Ann Arbor, 1937, p. 278, Figs. 23–5.

[6] Sir Harry Garner, *Oriental Blue and White*, London, 1954, Plate 10 (Chinese); Pope, *Ardebil*, Plate 11 (Chinese); *The Godman Collection of Oriental and Spanish Pottery and Glass*, London, 1901, Plate 7 (Syrian jar).

(1) *Plate* 13B; (2) *Plate* 16A.

FIFTEENTH-CENTURY BLUE-AND-WHITE

Egypt

No Egyptian blue-and-white vessels survive intact, but the fragments found at Fustāt suggest that before the end of the fourteenth century the local 'panel style' had begun to go out of fashion. Potters now painted and signed their wares in blue, especially the Ghaibī workshop mentioned in the previous chapter.[1] Ghaibī's name occurs on pieces painted with the symmetrical growing lotus design, but is more commonly associated with a spray bearing a pair of peaches or pomegranates—a Chinese motive very popular on porcelain with the reign-mark of Hsüan Tê (1426–35).[2] Swimming ducks and flying birds, much stylized, are isolated from their accompanying ornament; and pairs of fish seem to derive from the relief-patterns on celadon rather than from blue-and-white originals. Apart from an occasional animal vivaciously painted in the Near-Eastern manner, the drawing and potting of the wares with Ghaibī's signature show a decline from fourteenth-century standards. It is just possible that this workshop continued operating until the sixteenth century, for a few pieces are painted in a polychrome palette, including pale green, aubergine, and ochre-yellow, that seems to link up with the Damascus tiles and vessels of the Ottoman period.[3] Blue-and-white signed by the potters Ghazāl, ash-Shāmī, and Ibn al-Khabbāz are generally inferior to those by Ghaibī. As in Syria, the fourteenth-century blue-and-black 'panel style' persisted also in Egypt, the fifteenth-century pieces being distinguished by their coarser make and drawing and by the large areas painted in solid black through which spiral-motives are incised with a sharp point. An outstanding example of this 'incised black' manner is a mosque-lamp in New York signed 'Ibn al-Ghaibī at-Tawrīzī' (the son of Ghaibī of Tabrīz) (l). The Fustāt fragments suggest that in the fifteenth century there was a revival of the pre-Mongol taste for painting in black under a transparent turquoise glaze, with or without incised detail. Black-and-turquoise seems indeed to have taken on a new lease of life in all countries of the Near East as a natural alternative to blue-and-white.

Persia

From Persia we have unfortunately only the scantiest material evidence to demonstrate the arrival of the blue-and-white fashion, and

[1] P. 19.
[2] *Philadelphia Exhibition*, nos. 54, 56, 61. M. Bahrami, 'Chinese porcelains from Ardebil,' *Oriental Ceramic Society Transactions*, vol. 25, London, 1949–50, Plate 1d (unmarked); Pope, *Ardebil*, Plate 49.
[3] P. 62.

(l) *Plate* 17A.

it must be admitted that somewhat disappointing results are given by another possible source of information—the illustrations of court scenes in datable Persian illuminated manuscripts.[1] No recognizable pottery vessels of any kind are shown in the great Il-Khan manuscripts of the first half of the fourteenth century—the contemporaries of the 'Sultānābād' pottery.[2] When the Il-Khan empire disintegrated after 1335 south Persia was dominated successively by rulers of the Inju and Muzaffarid families, under whom a provincial and old-fashioned school of miniature-painters worked at Shīrāz. No blue-and-white appears in the four Shīrāzī manuscripts that bear dates between 1330 and 1370; nor do they appear in an *'Ajā'ib al-Makhlūqāt* (Wonders of the World) written at Baghdad in 1388 for Ahmad the Jalairid (1382–1410), a prince who ruled over north-west Persia and Mesopotamia with intervals caused by the invasions of Timur. In fact the earliest manuscript that shows blue-and-white vessels was one written for the same Ahmad the Jalairid at Baghdad in 1396—the beautiful copy of the poems of Khwājū Kirmāni in the British Museum.[3] One miniature of a garden-scene shows a table on which stand three pear-shaped bottles with spreading mouth; two of these are painted in blue-and-white, the third with a white dragon on a solid blue ground. The last quite possibly belonged to a rare class of Chinese fourteenth-century blue-glazed porcelain with decoration in raised white relief.[4] After 1400 blue-and-white vessels are so frequently shown in the manuscripts painted for the successors of Timur that there can be no doubt of their wide currency in Persia. They are almost invariably decorated with Chinese subjects such as the dragon and phoenix (gold vessels in the same miniatures have Islamic ornament): but their shapes are often so unlike any existing Chinese or Persian blue-and-white vessels that we cannot accept the drawings as accurate. They are probably confections of the painters' memory or imagination. Very few dated manuscripts of the second half of the fourteenth century survive, so the evidence of the 1396 Khwājū Kirmāni is not to be regarded as a significant *post quem*.

Between 1380 and 1404 Persia was periodically convulsed by the furious countermarches of Timur the Lame, in quest of blood and

[1] A. L. B. Ashton, 'Early Blue and White in Persian MSS,' in *Oriental Ceramic Society Transactions*, London, 1934–5, pp. 21–5. Basil Gray, 'Blue and White Vessels in Persian Miniatures of the Fourteenth and Fifteenth Centuries,' *op. cit.*, vol. 24, 1948–9, pp. 23–30.

[2] See pp. 4, 5.

[3] Douglas Barrett, *Persian painting of the fourteenth century*, London, 1952, Plate 8. Ashton, *op. cit.*, Plate 7.

[4] John Ayers, 'Some wares of the Yüan dynasty,' *Oriental Ceramic Society Transactions*, vol. 29, 1954–5.

glory. He carried off hundreds of artisans to beautify his capital at Samarqand, among them the tile-makers who made the admirable glazed revetments and tile-mosaic in Timurid buildings in that city and in Bukhāra. Timur died in 1404, on his way at the age of seventy-one to conquer China. Throughout the fifteenth century his descendants ruled over most of Persia from their seats of government at Herāt, Samarqand and Bukhāra. In the borderlands to the west, the rival Black Sheep and White Sheep Turkoman dynasties pursued an ancient feud, with Tabrīz as the prize. The Timurid princes were great patrons of art, especially miniature-painting, and their interest in China is attested by the famous embassy which Shāh Rukh (1404–1447), the son of Timur, sent to the Emperor Yung Lo in 1419–22.[1] Under the Timurids the grammar of Persian ornament, which had already been given a Chinese inflexion by the Mongols, set more firmly into a conventional Persian-Chinese idiom.[2] The lotus, cloud-scrolls, dragons and kylins filled out, merging with native arabesques into a scheme of softly undulating curves, at once more voluptuous and less exciting than the nervous angularity of true Chinese work. This Timurid style apparently prevailed among the painters, weavers and tile-makers[3] long before it reached the potters, who first used it to good effect in Turkey during the sixteenth century.

It might appear from our scanty evidence, which may be deceptive, that the fifteenth century was a bad time for pottery in Persia, and the sixteenth perhaps not very much better. Roughly-made peasant-wares whose variety defies classification show the bankruptcy of the fourteenth-century 'Sultānābād' styles.[4] The lustre-painted wares of Kāshān were almost extinct.[5] Blue-and-white Chinese porcelain must have been available before the end of the fourteenth century (there are some thirty pieces of that date in the Ardebīl collection), and it

[1] Discussed above, p. 27.

[2] This spread to Turkey, where it was known as the *hatāyī* ('Cathayan' i.e. Chinese) style.

[3] Especially in 'tile-mosaic' and *cuerda seca* tile-work (p. 42), of which important early examples showing the Timurid style are in the Gur Emir, or Mausoleum of Timur at Samarqand (about 1404); the 'Blue Mosque' at Tabrīz, completed in 1465 by Jāhān Shāh of the Black Sheep Turcoman; and the 'Green Mosque' and 'Green Tomb' at Bursa in Turkey, built between 1419 and 1424.

[4] Well discussed by G. Reitlinger, 'The Interim Period in Persian Pottery,' *Ars Islamica*, vol. 5, Ann Arbor, 1938, pp. 155–78; and *idem*, 'Sultānābād,' in *Oriental Ceramic Society Transactions*, vol. 20, London, 1944–5, pp. 25–34.

[5] Very late examples are tomb-slabs dated 886 H/1481–2 A.D.; 891 H/1486 A.D. (M. Bahrami, 'Some Examples of Il-Khanid Art,' in *Bulletin of the American Institute for Iranian Art and Archaeology*, vol. 5, New York, 1938, p. 260, Fig. 4. Florence Day, 'Review of A Survey of Persian Art,' in *Ars Islamica*, vol. 8, Ann Arbor, 1941, p. 56.) Late lustre vessels, Reitlinger, *op. cit.*, 'Sultānābād,' Plate 15*c, d*.

should have inspired a revival of pottery in Persia. One would look for early Persian blue-and-white at the Timurid capitals, Herāt and Samarqand, but so far almost none has been reported.[1] The fifteenth-century cities are still inhabited, so that excavation is difficult; moreover the dealers have probably thought that pieces of this late date would not be worth rescuing for western collectors. We have at present only isolated examples to represent what may have been a fairly extensive production. The bowl in Plate 18 is a strange hybrid; the flying bird in the central medallion suggests the last gasp of the Kāshān lustre style, and other unquestionably Chinese motives have been deformed and simplified. Another bowl (1), said to come from Sāva, is more finely potted; its painting in bright blue quite credibly evokes the spirit, if not the detail, of a Chinese bowl of the Hsüan Tê period (1426–35). In the Royal Scottish Museum, Edinburgh, is a cut-down globular spittoon inscribed under the base 'completed in Meshed of the Imām Rezā for Mawlānā Hesām al-Dīn of Shīrāz 848' (= 1444 A.D.); it is of soft white material, discoloured to brown, and though the floral decoration is in a Chinese style very similar to that on the bowl in Plate 19, it is painted in opaque underglaze green instead of blue.[2] Perhaps this piece will one day serve as a clue to identify other early wares made at Meshed, which is believed to have been an important ceramic centre in the seventeenth century.

It is not until the second half of the fifteenth century that we can pick up a thread in Persia that leads onwards unbroken for at least a hundred and fifty years. It consists of a technically homogeneous class of pottery (2) which goes under the name of Kubachi—a remote hill-town of Daghestan in the Caucasus, where a great many intact pieces, mostly plates and dishes, were found. The inhabitants had evidently acquired them in exchange for the steel weapons which they made locally and traded to Persia. They considered these possessions too valuable for common use, so pierced holes in their foot-rings and suspended them as house-decoration on the walls, where they remained to attract the attention of Russian and other antique-dealers

---

[1] The large fragment-collection from Afrasiyāb, near Samarqand, in the Victoria and Albert Museum, mainly of ninth-eleventh-century date, contains two Persian blue-and-white dish-fragments which might date from the fifteenth century. They are of very good quality and from very big dishes. See p. 99 for a notice of an artist-potter at Herāt in the late fifteenth century.

[2] This piece was brought to my attention by Revel Oddy. An opaque green, probably derived from iron, is found on Egyptian pottery of the fourteenth and fifteenth centuries, and was used for painting on the Kirmān polychrome ware of the seventeenth.

---

(1) *Plate* 19; (2) *Plates* 20, 21, 52–6.

in the last century.[1] The dirt of ages is still found as a hard brown crust on the backs of many of the vessels, deeply staining the edge of the foot where it is unprotected by the glaze. From Persia itself come tiles, whose provenance is unrecorded, and a few fragmentary or weather-worn vessels found in excavations. It is said that many fragments were found at Sāva, but no kiln-wasters to prove local manufacture. It is tempting to conjecture that the ware was made at Tabrīz, which lies across the natural approach to the Caucasus and would also be exposed to the possible Turkish influence that became evident in the Kubachi polychrome-painted pottery towards the end of the sixteenth century. Potters of Tabrīz origin, and perhaps trained there, attained distinction by their work in Egypt and Turkey.[2] But so far no important finds of pottery have been reported from Tabrīz, and current opinion in Persia discounts its claim to be a ceramic centre. For the present, then, it will be better to retain the nickname 'Kubachi' as a convenient label.

The technical characteristics of the 'Kubachi' ware remain constant over a very long period, though different colour-schemes are used for the painting. The white body is exceptionally soft, loose-grained, and porous; the brilliant glaze is thin, rather uneven, and very prone to develop a wide-meshed crackle. Grease and other dirt seeps in through the cracks and often discolours the underlying body to an even pale brownish tint. The early imitations of Chinese blue-and-white dishes are heavily potted, like the originals, but other vessels feel rather flimsy and are light in weight for their size. It gives the impression of being a somewhat rough ware, handsomely redeemed by the peculiarly attractive touch of the painting. This is always very sketchy, but shows an unerring grasp of decorative rhythm; in sixteenth-century pieces especially the freehand effect is in marked contrast to the calculated precision of the contemporary Turkish wares.

The earliest documented 'Kubachi' specimens are four flat-rimmed plates with well-developed fairly narrow foot-rings, painted in intense black under a pale turquoise glaze. On the one illustrated here (1)

---

[1] See The Hon. John Abercromby, *A Trip through the Eastern Caucasus*, London, 1899, pp. 253 ff. Also Arthur Lane, 'The so-called "Kubachi" wares of Persia,' *Burlington Magazine*, vol. 75, London, 1939, pp. 156–62. In the same way quantities of Turkish Isnik ware survived till modern times in the houses of the thrifty Greeks at Lindos in the island of Rhodes (p. 60).

[2] Ghaibī in Egypt signs himself 'es-Shāmī' or 'at-Tawrīzī'; it may have been his son who signed the mosque-lamp, Plate 17A, 'ibn al-Ghaibī at-Tawrīzī' (p. 31). 'The Masters of Tabrīz' collectively signed glazed tilework in the Green Mosque at Bursa about 1424 (p. 42).

(1) *Plate* 20A.

there is a concentric inscription reading 'May this dish ever be full and surrounded by friends, may they never lack anything and eat their fill', with the date 873 H/1469 A.D. Others have dates equivalent to 1473, 1480, and 1495. The most immediately striking feature of the decoration is the black ground through which running spiral patterns have been incised with a sharp point—a procedure widespread in fifteenth-century Islamic pottery.[1] The plant sprays in the reserved ogee panels and medallions are stunted adaptations of those on Chinese blue-and-white porcelain of the early fifteenth century, and the bowl, Plate 20B, has Chinese lotus-panels on the outside.[2] The turquoise-and-black colour scheme is still found on 'Kubachi' vessels which, to judge from their changing style of decoration and shapes, range throughout the sixteenth century into the first half of the seventeenth. A few heavily constructed dishes with the wide Chinese foot and wavy edge are painted with pairs of fish or birds under a bright yellowish green (1),[3] but these are almost certainly to be dated after 1500. Other heavy dishes of the same typically Chinese shape are painted in a strong warm blue with designs fairly closely imitated from Chinese porcelain of the early fifteenth century (2)—rock-and-wave border, coiled lotus- and chrysanthemum-sprays, and an undulating lotus-wreath on the reverse round the convex bulge of the well.[4] These again are probably later than they look, after 1500, and it seems that there are few or no survivors of the 'Kubachi' blue-and-white that must have been made in the fifteenth century. A possible candidate is a large globular ewer in the Victoria and Albert Museum (neck and handle missing), with lotus-panels, rock-and-wave, and lotus-flowers wildly painted in a strong runny blue. The 'Kubachi' pieces of the sixteenth and early seventeenth century will be discussed elsewhere.[5]

---

[1] Compare the Egyptian mosque-lamp, Plate 17A.

[2] A similar bowl with Chinese fruit design illustrated in *C. L. Davids Samling, Nogle Studier*, Copenhagen, 1948, p. 105.

[3] One with a floral spray illustrated, *C. L. Davids Samling, Nogle Studier*, Copenhagen, 1948, p. 103.

[4] Compare *Philadelphia Exhibition Catalogue*, nos. 37, 38; Sir Harry Garner, *Oriental Blue and White*, Plate 14.

[5] Pp. 78–81, 92–3.

---

(1) *Plate* 52A; (2) *Plate* 21A.

3

TURKISH POTTERY

General

According to the Shāh Nāmāh, the epic Book of Kings, Turān was the country east of the Oxus River: the Turks who dwelt there were Persia's ancient enemies, and Rustam slew their King Afrasiyāb. Historically, Transoxiana was conquered by the Umayyad Caliph Walīd I at the beginning of the eighth century, and thoroughly converted to Islam by its Persian rulers of the Samanid house in the ninth and tenth. But the bleak steppes of Turkestan to the north-east bred a hardy nomad race in greater numbers than the pasture could sustain, and smaller or larger bands continually drifted into the cultivated territories to the west. At the beginning of the eleventh century the Turkish adventurer Mahmūd of Ghazna carved out a great empire for himself in South Persia, Afghanistan and India. Even more important were the Seldjuk Turks who moved into Persia after his death, chasing out the petty dynasts of Islam until they had established their own ascendancy from the Oxus to the Mediterranean. In 1055 the Great Seldjuk Toghril Beg did homage to the Caliph at Baghdad and in return was invested as Sultan of the East and West. In Persia and Mesopotamia the Seldjuk Empire passed away with the death of Sultan Sanjar in 1157, but meanwhile the tribe had advanced the frontiers of Islam in a direction where the Arab conquerors had never been able to settle. In 1071, at Manzikert in Armenia, Toghril Beg's nephew Alp Arslān decisively defeated the Byzantine Emperor Romanus Diogenes, thus laying open the approaches of southern Asia Minor (Anatolia). A distinct Seldjuk Empire of Rūm (i.e. Rome) maintained itself with varying fortune in Anatolia from 1078 till the ruling family died out in 1300. The Seldjuks encroached further on Byzantine territory to the north, capturing Nicaea (Isnik), and under Kilij Arslān I they harassed the First Crusaders on their way from Byzantium to Antioch in 1197. Soon after they sealed off this land approach to the Holy Land. Under 'Alā al-Dīn Kai Kubad I (1219–36) the Seldjuk Empire reached its greatest prosperity with its capital at Konya. In 1243 Ghiyāth al-Dīn Kai Khusrau II was forced to do homage to the Mongols in face of invasion, but Anatolia remained free from permanent Mongol occupation all through the thirteenth century. It thus became a place of refuge for scholars and artists who could no longer work in Persia. They greatly enriched the art and culture of their new home.

At the time of Jenghiz Khan's first Persian invasion, a small tribe of Turks then living in Khorāsān decided to emigrate to Anatolia (1224). Here their successive leaders Suleymān and Ertoghrul became trusted lieutenants of the Seldjuks in their war against the Byzantines. When the Seldjuks died out, the tribe now led by 'Osmān gradually emerged victorious over the other Turkish succession-states. The Osmanli or Ottoman dynasty in fact dates its beginning from 1300. Bursa (Brussa) became its first capital in 1329. 'Osmān's successor Orhan was the first to carry war across the Dardanelles into Europe, where in 1355 he captured Edirne (Adrianople) and made it his new capital. The triumphant career of Bayezid I Ilderim ('the Thunderbolt') ended disastrously with his defeat and capture by Timur at the battle of Ankara in 1402; but Ottoman fortunes were restored by his son Mehmed I Celebi ('the Gentleman'). In 1453 Mehmed II Fatih ('the Conqueror') stormed Constantinople and annihilated the oldest Empire in history: the Byzantine-Roman power that had lasted through fourteen centuries from the time of Augustus. With the Sultan in the palace of the Caesars and the crescent on the dome of Haghia Sophia, Christian Europe now faced a danger greater than the Mongols. Istanbul became the capital of an Empire which in the sixteenth century spread over south-east Europe and round the whole eastern and southern shores of the Mediterranean, where it survived into living memory. For our present purpose, particular importance attaches to the conquest by Selim I ('the Grim') of Syria in 1516 and Egypt in the next year. The Ottomans there effaced the Mamluks who had defeated the Crusaders and survived for almost three centuries as the most stable Islamic power in the Near East. Under Suleyman I 'the Magnificent' (1520–66) Turkey played one of the leading roles in European power-politics. Only in Persia could the Ottomans make no appreciable headway; under its Safavid Shahs that country had become a nation which in the sixteenth and seventeenth centuries was capable of holding its own.

There were two main periods in the history of what is still called Turkey when the arts particularly flourished. Under the Seldjuks of Rūm (1078–1300) it was the thirteenth century, when the capital was at Konya. Under the Ottomans (1300–1918) some notable buildings were erected at Bursa and Edirne in the first half of the fifteenth century, but the most lavish development accompanied the foundation of new mosques and palaces in Istanbul during the sixteenth century.

Seldjuk tilework and pottery: thirteenth century

The thirteenth-century mosques and religious colleges at Konya are remarkable for their elaborately carved stone façades and for the mosaics of glazed tilework that cover their interior walls and vaults.[1] In the mosque of 'Alā al-Dīn (1220) the technique of this tile-mosaic is already mature, and as no earlier buildings in Persia have anything that can be closely compared with it, the invention seems likely to have been first worked out on Turkish soil. It may nevertheless be the handiwork of Persian craftsmen, for the material of the tiles is the same white ground quartz composition as was used for fine pottery in Persia, Syria and Egypt since the middle of the twelfth century, and this could hardly have been discovered independently in a country with no previous ceramic tradition. After Jenghiz Khan's first Mongol invasion in 1219 many more Persians must have fled to Anatolia, and tile-mosaic in the Sircali Medrese at Konya (1243) actually bears the signature of a Persian, Muhammad the son of Muhammad, the son of Othmān, from Tūs in Khorāsān.[2] Tile-mosaic resembles a jig-saw puzzle in that the patterns are fitted together with coloured pieces of tile specially cut to shape. The pieces were sawn from slabs already glazed and fired, and laid face downwards on a cartoon of the whole design. A thick layer of liquid plaster was then poured over the back, settling in the bevels between the pieces; canes set crossways in the plaster strengthened it to form a panel which could be lifted and fixed in position against the wall. Stars, intersecting bands and other straight-edged geometric motives predominate in the Seldjuk tile-mosaic, but there are also curvilinear arabesque and bold Kufic inscriptions. The chief colours are purple-black, pale turquoise, blue, white, and in the later examples, a certain amount of yellow-brown. On the lower part of the walls, bands of mosaic are used to frame large panels of hexagonal turquoise or blue tiles each stencilled with a self-contained arabesque pattern in unfired gold. The general effect is harsh but very impressive, matching the barbaric vigour of the stone-carvings outside the buildings.

Tile-mosaic is purely architectural, but evidence is now forthcoming that the tile-makers used other techniques equally suitable for decorating pottery vessels. Of the palace at Konya only one ruined pavilion survived till recent times. Its walls were covered with

[1] See especially F. Sarre, *Denkmäler persischer Baukunst*, Berlin, 1901–10, pp. 120–43, Plates 89–109.
[2] S. P. and H. C. Seherr-Thoss, *Design and Colour in Islamic Architecture, Afghanistan, Iran, Turkey*, Washington, 1968, Plates 119, 120.

variously-shaped tiles painted in *mināī* enamel colours and gold, like a class of Persian pottery.[1] An inscription with the name of Kilij Arslān probably refers to the fourth ruler of that name (1257–67). In a Seldjuk palace recently excavated at Kubādābād, on the western shore of Lake Beysehir, there were quantities of star- and cross-tiles painted either in yellowish lustre on a white or blue glaze, or in black, blue and purple underglaze colours.[2] In style, the first group resembles the lustre-painted pottery of Rayy in Persia; the second recalls the underglaze-painted wares of Raqqa in Northern Mesopotamia. Potters from both those places may have come to Anatolia to make them, for the rather poor technique has peculiarities that argue for a local origin. Similar tiles have been found elsewhere in Anatolia, at Antalya, Alara, and Alanya.[3] Our natural expectation that the tile-makers also produced pottery vessels is confirmed by fragments with lustre or underglaze painting discovered at Konya, but so far no reasonably complete examples have been found. Indeed the industry seems to have struck no deep roots in Anatolia, either for lack of encouragement or because the local materials were not thought satisfactory. By far the commonest pottery found on Seldjuk sites is lead-glazed sgraffiato-ware, of types current in the Crusader settlements to the south and the Byzantine dominions to the north. We do not at present know for certain whether this was also made in Seldjuk territory.

With the end of the Seldjuk dynasty of Rūm in 1300 the arts entered a long period of eclipse. The mihrāb of the mosque at Birge (1312) was the last major work by the makers of tile-mosaic; their craft then died out in Turkey, and more than a hundred years were to pass before it was reintroduced from abroad. Even the procedure for making the white ground-quartz material was forgotten.

Early Ottoman pottery and tilework: fifteenth century

During this dark period, while the Ottomans were ranging after power, a robust but unpretentious type of painted pottery gained wide

---

[1] F. Sarre, *Der Kiosk von Konya*, Berlin, 1936, pp. 14–22, Plates 4–7.

[2] Zeki Oral, 'Kubad Ābād cinileri,' in *Turk Tarih Kurumu Belleten*, vol. 18, no. 66, Ankara, 1953, pp. 209–22.

[3] Rudolf M. Riefstahl, 'Turkish Architecture in Southwest Anatolia,' *Art Studies*, vol. 8, Princeton, 1930–1, pp. 144–5, Figs. 97, 98 (Antalya). Fragments from the other two sites have been recovered by Dr. D. S. Rice. Tiles of both groups were also found in excavations at the Keykubadiye Kiosk near Kayseri attributed like the palace at Kubādābād to 'Ala al-Dīn Keykubād (1220–1237); tiles of the second group have been found in the Ortokid palace at Diyarbekr attributed to the thirteenth century: O. Aslanapa, 'Türkische Fliesen und Keramik in Anatolien,' *Türk Kültürünü Arastirma Enstitüsü Yayinlari*, 10, Istanbul, 1965, p. 14 and Figs. 5–8 and plates 4–10 (in colour).

currency in Anatolia (1). For long called 'Miletus' ware, it is now known to have been made at Isnik where kiln evidence was discovered in excavations carried out in 1963 and 1964.[1] Unlike the other pottery discussed in this book, it is ordinary earthenware, of coarse red clay with a white slip and a clear lead-glaze covering the painted decoration. This is usually in sombre dark blue with black outlines and touches of purple; less often in blue or green alone. The typical convex bowls and deep dishes sometimes have an offset lip, and the glaze on the back is often stained green; it leaves the substantial foot exposed. Some pieces have geometrical or radiating designs (1) recalling the international 'panel style' of the fourteenth century. A favourite treatment shows a central rosette and concentric bands of gadroons, with a border-pattern crudely imitating the 'wave and rock' of Chinese fourteenth-century blue-and-white porcelain, which also inspired some broadly drawn plant-motives. The areas of solid blue or black often have spirals or cable-patterns incised through them with a sharp point. In all these characteristics the 'Miletus-ware' has stylistic affinities with the peasant-wares of Persia and the coarser Syrian and Egyptian wares of the fifteenth century, from which it differs in its earthenware material. It should date mainly from the first half of the fifteenth century, hardly earlier. A purely Islamic provincial type, showing no traces of Byzantine influence in style, it disappears abruptly without any relation to the fine pottery developed at Isnik towards the end of the fifteenth century.

As has been mentioned above, the Ottoman power narrowly escaped destruction when Timur invaded Anatolia and captured Bayezid I at the battle of Ankara in 1402. Bayezid's sons fought among themselves until Mehmed I gained the mastery from his base at Bursa. This beautiful city, on a mountain side above a smiling plain of orchards, vineyards, and cypresses, contains the first major monuments of Ottoman art—the Yesil Cami (Green Mosque) completed between 1419 and 1424; and the Yesil Turbe, the adjoining mausoleum completed after Mehmed's death in 1421.[2] Murad II (1421–51) built at Bursa another mosque and the earliest of several *turbes* where members of the Ottoman family lie buried, but his finest construction was the

[1] F. Sarre, 'Die Keramik der islamischer Zeit von Milet,' in *Milet*, etc., ed. Th. Wiegand, vol. 3, *Das islamische Milet*, Berlin, 1935, pp. 69 ff. For excavations at Isnik, see O. Aslanapa, *op. cit.*, pp. 29–32 and Figs. 4–64 and Plates 12–31 (in colour).

[2] The best illustrations in L. Parvillée, *Architecture et décoration turques au XV siècle*, Paris, 1874: and Celal Esad Arseven, *L'art turc*, Istanbul, 1939, and *Les arts décoratifs turcs*, Istanbul, 1952: and S. P. and H. C. Seherr-Thoss, *op. cit.*, Plates 121–4.

(1) *Plate* 17B.

Muradiye Mosque at Edirne (1435). The Green Mosque and Tomb took their name from the turquoise-glazed tiles on their outer walls. Inside, the decoration is of extraordinary richness. The lower walls are panelled with turquoise, blue or green hexagonal tiles, on which are stencilled gold patterns. The *mihrāb* (prayer-niche) and surrounding wall are covered to a height of about thirty feet with a complex tile-work composition in which the principal motives are Kufic or *neskhi* inscriptions, arabesques, and smoothly undulating plant ornaments of Persian-Chinese character. This is in fact the ornament associated in Persia with Timur and his descendants;[1] and the Green Mosque significantly marks the introduction of the Timurid-Persian style into Turkey. An inscription on the tiles of the *mihrāb* says 'Made by the Masters of Tabrīz'; another on tiles in the Sultan's gallery reads 'Made by Muhammad al-Majnūn' ('Muhammad the Mad', in Persian); a third, on the carved wooden doors of the Green Tomb, 'Made by 'Alī ibn-Hājjī Ahmed of Tabrīz'.[2] A painted inscription on stone over the Sultan's gallery in the Mosque says 'The decoration of this holy building was completed by the meanest of men, 'Alī ibn-Ilyas 'Alī, in 827 H' (A.D. 1424). This man appears to have been the overseer in charge of the whole of the decorations; he is otherwise known in Turkish history as 'The Painter' Naqqāsh 'Alī, a native of Bursa who as a boy was carried off to Transoxiana by Timur in 1402. He evidently became familiar with the Timurid style in Samarqand and Tabrīz, and was no doubt the intermediary through whom a gang of Persian craftsmen was assembled in Tabrīz to come and work in Bursa. The more elaborate parts of the tile-decorations are in two distinct techniques; one pure tile-mosaic, the other a less exacting substitute which aimed at a similar effect by painting the designs in thick coloured glazes on to large slabs of earthenware. The glazes were prevented from running together in their molten state by outlining the patterns in a dark, greasy pigment, which burned dry and confined them in their proper areas; the same technique was used by the Moorish tile-makers in Spain, where it is known as *cuerda seca* ('dry cord'). For all their richness, the colours of the Bursa tilework lack the brilliance of the earlier Seldjuk tile-mosaic; this is partly because the transparent glazes were laid on a body of red potter's clay (the body of the contemporary 'Miletus-ware'), and not on a white composition of ground quartz.

The tilework in the Mosque of Murad II at Edirne (1435) is if anything richer than that of Bursa, though its style is so similar that it

---

[1] See p. 33.

[2] F. Taeschner, 'Die Jesil Gami in Brussa,' in *Der Islam*, vol. 20, Berlin and Leipzig, 1932, pp. 139–68, especially 166–8.

must have been made by the same company of Persian craftsmen. But in the meanwhile the company had added a new technique to their repertory; tiles of white material, with underglaze painting in blue-and-white or in black under turquoise. Specially shaped tiles thus painted are incorporated with the tile-mosaic and *cuerda seca* decorations of the *mihrāb*; others, of hexagonal shape, form a dado elsewhere in the mosque. The blue-and-white designs, largely inspired by those on Chinese porcelain, are so close to those on almost contemporary tiles in Damascus as to make it appear highly probable that a number of Syrian potters had attached themselves to the Persian company working at Edirne.[1] In the Uc Serefeli Cami (Mosque of the Three Balconies) at Edirne, built between 1437–47, is more tilework that could be attributed to the Syrians: two pointed panels over windows in the courtyard have inscriptions and background-foliage painted in underglaze blue, turquoise and purple, with black outlines. After this the potters may have gone home, for to judge from extant monuments a long period intervened before tiles with underglaze painting in a very different style re-appeared on Turkish buildings. We have no evidence at all to suggest that the putative Syrians made any pottery vessels on Turkish soil. It is moreover doubtful whether the Persian *cuerda seca* technique became permanently naturalized there; at the mosque of Mehmed II the Conqueror in Istanbul are two very fine panels dating from the original building of 1463–71, but the decorations of the Cinili Kösk (1472) are confined to tile-mosaic and gold-stencilled tiles, and the Mosque of Bayezid II (1500–5) had no tile-decorations at all. In the Mosque and Turbe of Selim I (1523) begins a new series of *cuerda seca* tiles, of whiter material and more radiant colours; they are very Persian in style and are almost certainly the work of a fresh band of immigrants from Persia. Selim I had captured Tabrīz in 1514, and contemporary sources are unanimous in saying that he carried off a great number of its artisans to Istanbul.

Isnik pottery I: the 'Abraham of Kutahya' style. About 1490–1525

From the account so far given it will be seen that for almost three centuries Turkey remained somewhat unpropitious for the

[1] Rudolf M. Riefstahl, 'Early Turkish Tile-revetments in Edirne,' in *Ars Islamica*, vol. 4, Ann Arbor, 1937, p. 268. Riefstahl believed that Persians from Tabrīz were responsible for introducing these blue-and-white tiles to both Syria and Turkey. I have given reasons for my different interpretation of the evidence in 'The Ottoman Pottery of Isnik,' *Ars Orientalis*, vol. 2, Ann Arbor, 1956, p. 252. The makers must have arrived after the Persians had done their work in the Green Mosque and Tomb at Bursa, where the only blue-and-white tiles are a few on the sarcophagus of a wife or daughter of Mehmed I who died at a later date. For the Syrian tiles, see p. 30 above and Plate 13B.

development of the potter's art. With the exception of the Seldjuk tile-mosaic, the enterprise begun by talented foreigners dwindled to nothing after one or two generations. It is therefore baffling to explain how Turkey at length gave birth to an indigenous ceramic industry more original and more productive than any other described in this book.

This industry was located at Isnik (the ancient Nicaea), which lies some sixty miles south-east from Istanbul across the Bosporus. Isnik pottery was famous in the sixteenth and seventeenth centuries; its name then passed into oblivion. Nineteenth-century collectors first called it 'Persian ware'; as further misinformation came to hand, they assigned the three main groups to Kutahya, Damascus, and the Island of Rhodes. These labels have stuck, and we may ourselves prefer to retain them as nicknames more convenient than 'Isnik I, II and III'.

The wares of the first, 'Kutahya', group are painted in blue-and-white (1). An initial clue to their date is given by an entry in the inventory of the Topkapu Serai Palace for 901 H/1495 A.D.—'spouted jugs (*ibriq*), and water-bowls (*ligen*) of Isnik'. The inventory for 910 H/1505 A.D. repeats this, and adds '10 bowls with foot, of Isnik china'. The spouted jug illustrated here in Plate 24A has under its foot an inscription and date in Armenian: 'This vessel commemorates Abraham of Kutahya, servant of God. In the year 959 (=A.D. 1510), on the 11th of March.' There are tiles painted in similar style in the *turbe* adjoining the Mosque of Mustafa Pasha at Gebze, built in 1520; and in the Valide Mosque at Manissa, built in 1522–3. We may therefore assume that the first Isnik style, that conveniently named after 'Abraham of Kutahya', dates approximately between 1490 and 1525.[1]

In technique these early pieces already show the consistent perfection typical of Isnik ware for at least a hundred years to come. It is easily the best pottery made in the Near East since the Kāshān wares of the thirteenth century. The white body, less compact and less hard than that of Kāshān, is obviously of the same character; it may contain a higher proportion of white clay to glassy matter. There is no attempt to make the walls translucent, as so often in the early Persian wares, and the potting is fairly robust. A dilute wash of the body-material—too thin to be called a slip—was sponged over the raw surface as a ground for the painting. The brilliant colourless glaze is very

[1] This and other questions are more fully discussed by the present writer in 'The Ottoman Pottery of Isnik,' *Ars Orientalis*, vol. 2, Ann Arbor, 1956, pp. 247–281. Katharina Otto-Dorn's *Das Islamische Iznik*, Berlin, 1941, contains an invaluable series of contemporary documents compiled by R. Anhegger. O. Aslanapa in the course of the excavations at Isnik recovered many fragments of the Isnik wares including masters. See O. Aslanapa's article in *Türk San'ati Tarihi Araştirma ve Incelemeleri*, vol. II (1969).

(1) *Plates* 22–8.

thin and close-fitting; it does not crackle or form into superfluous drops like that on the fifteenth-century Edirne tiles or most Syrian pottery, and it covers the whole surface except for the edge of the foot-ring. The blue used for painting on some pieces is sombre and blackish—perhaps an indication of their relatively early date within the group. Usually the colour is warm and brilliant, being skilfully laid in shades of varying strength. Panels and other areas rather unaccountably left white among the crowded designs were probably painted in unfired gold which has since worn off; traces of the gold still remain on tiles of this class in the Turbe of Prince Mahmūd at Bursa.[1] The tradition of gold painting on tiles in Turkey runs back continuously to Seldjuk times. The only other colour used is a very pale turquoise applied in sparing touches on a few pieces which for stylistic reasons must be the latest of the group. The whole technique is so superior to that of contemporary wares made in other countries that it would be hard to suggest a source whence it could have been introduced into Turkey.

There are indications that the Isnik craftsmen had little if any previous experience of making pots. Many of their shapes betray, by sharp articulations and finely profiled mouldings, an immediate derivation from vessels of metal. The jar on Plate 23A, perhaps the earliest of the group to survive, has two torus mouldings at the top and bottom of the neck, and two more round the foot—exactly like the contemporary Persian tankards of inlaid brass.[2] There are similar mouldings round the foot of the typical large 'bowls with foot' (as mentioned in the 1495 and 1505 inventories) (I). The metallic origin of the spouted ewer (*ibriq*) in Plate 24A is self-evident, and others have rectangular bodies with supporting knob-feet at the corners. The pen-box, Plate 25B, is directly translated from a metal example.[3] As time went on, and the potters discovered forms more appropriate to their own material, the sharp metallic excrescences were smoothed away. The mosque-lamp in Plate 24B probably belongs with four others in Istanbul to a set made for the Turbe of Bayezid II, who died in 1512. Its squat and angular profile may be compared with the more graceful

---

[1] Plate 23C probably came from this building.

[2] Persian tankards dated 1461 and 1511 in A. U. Pope (ed.), *A Survey of Persian Art*, London and New York, 1938, Plate 1376A, B. An undated silver-gilt Turkish tankard is in the Victoria and Albert Museum, no. 158—1894; it retains its dragon handle, which may be compared with our Plate 24A.

[3] Islamic metal pen-boxes were also imitated in early Ming porcelain. Sir Percival David, 'Chinese Porcelain at Constantinople,' *Oriental Ceramic Society Transactions*, no. 11, London, 1933–4, Plate 9. Basil Gray, 'The Influence of Near Eastern Metalwork on Chinese Ceramics,' *op. cit.*, no. 18, 1940–1, Plate 5C.

(I) *Plate* 26.

curves of a lamp only slightly later in date (Plate 25A).[1] Only two shapes obviously derive from Chinese blue-and-white porcelain—the large dish with wide footring and flat indented rim, and the rimless dish (I).

In spite of the blue-and-white colour scheme, the decoration of these Isnik wares of about 1490–1525 suggests that their makers had very little first-hand knowledge of Chinese porcelain, or even of Syrian imitations. The Serai inventories of 1495 and 1505 already quoted point to a scarcity of Chinese porcelain in Turkey before the conquests of Sultan Selim I in 1514–17.[2] If we concede that there is real Chinese feeling in the wreath on the back of the early dish, Plate 22, this is hardly true of the friezes at the top and bottom of the early jar, Plate 23A. The stylised cable-pattern on the neck of this jar is a motive that could have borrowed from the engraved ornament on a metal vase of the kind that inspired the shape.[3] But the rest of the ornament has a suppleness that would be impossible in engraving on metal. The painting on all vessels of the 'Abraham of Kutahya' class is conceived in terms of small, very detailed patterns carefully mapped out in bands, medallions, or panels of ornate contour. Patterns dark on light and light on dark contrast with each other in adjacent areas or on the inside and outside of a bowl. It is not a style naturally suited to the decoration of pottery, and stands far removed in spirit from the broad, freehand painting on the early fifteenth-century tiles at Edirne. In fact the immediate origin of the individual motives, and of the dense manner in which they are combined, is rather to be sought in contemporary Ottoman illuminated manuscripts. The surviving leaves from a magnificent Koran, formerly in the Mosque of Bayezid II at Istanbul, should be considered in conjunction with the pottery lamps made for the Turbe adjoining the same mosque.[4] We must conclude that the Isnik potters either had access to miniatures which they imitated, or that they were supplied with actual designs prepared by

[1] Mosque-lamps in pierced metal and glass have a long history. When made of pottery they can only have been hung as decoration—except perhaps for those made without a bottom (Plate 38).

[2] P. 28.

[3] Compare an engraved gilt-brass candlestick in the Museum of Turkish and Islamic Art, Istanbul, inscribed with the name of Bayezid II (1481–1512); illustrated in *Splendeur de l'art turc*, Paris, Musée des Arts Décoratifs, Exposition février-avril 1953, Plate 10, no. 140.

[4] F. R. Martin, *The Miniature Painting and Painters of Persia, India and Turkey*, London, 1912, Plates 264–272. The Mosque was built 1500–5; the date of the Turbe is uncertain, but the building and its fittings were probably completed after Bayezid's death in 1512. Pottery lamps from the Turbe are illustrated by A. Lane, 'The Ottoman pottery of Isnik,' *Ars Orientalis*, vol. 2., Ann Arbor, 1956, Figs. 16–18. The lamp here illustrated, Plate 24B, must belong to the same series.

(I) *Plates* 22, 29B.

the court miniature-painters in Istanbul. There is documentary evidence for this practice later in the sixteenth century.[1]

The motives of design fall into the two broad groups traditionally described by the Turks as *rūmī* and *hatāyī*. *Rūmī*, literally 'Roman', simply means Anatolian or Turkish, for the Seldjuks gave this name to the land which they conquered from the Byzantine Roman Empire in the eleventh century. *Rūmī* ornaments are in fact traditional arabesques based on the long, pointed leaf, which often has a second lobe branching from its curved side, often has a prehensile tip, and is always carried on intersecting stems with little tendrils derived ultimately from the classical vine.[2] The Turks had a fondness for plaiting the stems into elaborate knots, and they also plaited the shafts of the archaistic Kufic inscriptions that consort so happily with the arabesques (1). *Hatāyī* ('of Cathay', or China) refers to the hybrid Persian-Chinese designs which we have already mentioned in discussing Persian art under Timur and his successors.[3] The principal motives are the Chinese lotus and stylized cloud-scroll. Generally speaking, the two classes of design are used as foils to each other, being segregated into adjoining bands or panels; the taut, wiry rhythm of the *rūmī* arabesque makes a telling contrast with the softer undulations of the *hatāyī*. But sometimes the two themes interpenetrate each other in a single frieze (2). The Persian decorators of the early fifteenth-century mosques at Bursa and Edirne had already made full use of both *rūmī* and *hatāyī*, and the idiom they introduced was still current in Turkey when the Isnik potters began work towards the end of the century. But certain Turkish provincialisms are to be noticed in the Isnik painting. The artists introduced fantastic minor elaborations into the single elements of their designs, such as the arabesque leaf; they gave it an inner structure of its own, which by skilful shading was made to appear almost three-dimensional (3). The Chinese lotus quite lost the appearance of a flower, becoming a cluster of fleshy volutes, from which a tongue might unexpectedly protrude through an orifice (4). This 'plastic' treatment appears most pronounced in the earliest pieces of the series. For it is to some extent possible to recognize a stylistic development through the thirty to forty years covered by the 'Abraham of Kutahya' group. The earliest pieces, dating from the end of the fifteenth century (5), are painted in a sombre dark blue, which

[1] A Firman of 977 H/1569 A.D. ordered tiles to be made in conformity with patterns sent to Isnik; similar orders followed in 1574 and 1590. K. Otto-Dorn, *Das islamische Iznik*, Berlin, 1941, pp. 161, 162, 169.
[2] Good examples in Plates 22, 23A.   [3] Pp. 33, 42.

(1) *Plate* 25B; (2) *Plate* 29B; (3) *Plates* 22A, 23A.
(4) *Plate* 24B; (5) *Plates* 22, 23A.

combined with the crowded designs and powerfully stylized arabesques gives them an austere and rather heavy effect. On the 'Abraham
of Kutahya' ewer, dated 1510 (1), the blue is lighter and warmer, and
the decoration more open; this gives a clue to other pieces probably
made a little earlier or later (2). On the mosque-lamp, Plate 25A, the
painting, in rather pale blue, has an airy lightness that already antici-
pates the so called 'Golden Horn' style of about 1530. On a series of
rather late dishes (3) the designs have become quite flat, with no suggestion of plastic modelling, and their perfunctory construction
suggests that the painters had begun to lose interest. The painting on
the rimless dish, Plate 29B, is in a class by itself, being so accomplished
and by Persian standards so 'correct' that it is tempting to attribute it
to a trained miniature-painter. The cell-diaper in the middle might
well have been suggested by a somewhat similar treatment in carved
Chinese celadon dishes, and the shape is certainly Chinese. The high-
footed bowl in Plate 27 is of a shape found also with painting in later
Isnik styles (4); there are no metallic mouldings on the foot; and a
significant innovation is the use of a very pale clear turquoise to outline the panels inside and to fill the centres of the flowers. There are
similar touches of turquoise on another large bowl (5) whose inside
decoration includes leaves with serrated edges—a first sign of the
limited naturalism characteristic of the second phase of Isnik pottery,
towards which these two bowls may be regarded as 'transitional'.

It is a singular fact that in their early days the Isnik potters made
very few tiles. This in itself is an argument against any link between
them and the presumably Syrian makers of the blue-and-white tiles
at Edirne in 1433. There are 'Abraham of Kutahya'-type tiles in two
of the Turbes adjoining the Mosque of Murad II at Bursa, and in both
the painted tiles are very long and narrow, forming borders to wide
fields of the usual hexagonal monochrome tiles (6). One Turbe is the
burial-place of Prince Mustafa, son of Mehmed II the Conqueror, who
died in 1474. One might be tempted to believe that both the building
and its tile-decorations date from that time; but if so, the tiles would
be twenty years earlier than the next earliest document for Isnik
pottery—the Topkapu Serai inventories for 1495. The style of the
painting, in bright warm blue, is actually rather like that of the
'Abraham of Kutahya' ewer dated 1510 (7). This Turbe contains the
sarcophagi of Ahmed son of Mehmed 1, two sons and a daughter of
Bayezid II (1481–1512), besides that of his brother Mustafa. The
second Turbe at Bursa contains the sarcophagus of Prince Mahmūd,

---

(1) *Plate* 24A; (2) *Plates* 24B, 25, 26; (3) *Plate* 28A; (4) *Plate* 37.
(5) *Plate* 28B; (6) *Plates* 23B, c; (7) *Plate* 24A.

C. *Turkish (Isnik); about* 1540–50. *Diam.* 14¾ *in.*
Victoria and Albert Museum. (*pages* 53, 56)

executed by his father Bayezid II for insubordination in 1506; the other burials here are those of Mahmūd's wife and three sons, who were murdered (according to Ottoman family custom) by their uncle Selim I 'the Grim' in 1513, shortly after his accession. Selim so greatly increased the population of the royal tombs at Bursa that piety may have induced him to embellish their appearance, so that both sets of tiles might date from about 1513. The latest documented examples of the 'Abraham of Kutahya' group of Isnik pottery are the tile-panels in two pointed tympana over doorways in the Valide Mosque at Manissa, built in 1522–3. The designs show central inscriptions surrounded by ornamental borders with typically small and crowded designs; they are very awkwardly arranged on the courses of long narrow tiles that fill the space. It looks as though the potters were accustomed to designing narrow borders and had not yet learnt to spread a large design convincingly over several adjacent tiles. In this their work at Manissa compares unfavourably with the excellent designs in *cuerda seca* tilework filling similarly shaped panels at the Mosque of Selim I in Istanbul (also made in 1523).[1] The Istanbul tiles may well have been made by some of the Persian artists carried off by Selim I when he captured Tabrīz in 1514. There is a tradition in Turkey, which goes back no further than the eighteenth-century historian Kucuk Celebizade, that in 1514 Selim I settled a number of Tabrīzi potters at Isnik. This is not borne out by any contemporary documents, and no fundamental change in the established Isnik style began till at least ten years later. The changes that took place after about 1525 were not inspired by the example of any Persian pottery—certainly not by the so-called 'Kubachi' pottery, which might have been made at or near Tabrīz.[2] They were introduced gradually, on the initiative of the Isnik potters themselves—a cosmopolitan community of Turkish subjects which certainly included Armenians, and perhaps also Persians and Greeks.

Isnik pottery II: the 'Damascus' style. About 1525–55

The chronological span of the second phase of Isnik pottery covers roughly the period 1525–55. Though the technique of body and glaze remains constant throughout, and many of the shapes continue almost unchanged, there is increasing variety in the painted designs and in their colour-schemes. It is in fact the most creative period of Turkish pottery. At first the colours were confined to blue with small touches of brilliant turquoise, and the rather formal designs included vestiges of the 'Abraham of Kutahya' style; but to the same phase belong a

[1] K. Otto-Dorn, *Das islamische Iznik*, Berlin, 1941, Plate 49, Fig. 1.
[2] See pp. 34–6, 78–81, 92–3.

number of pieces quite faithfully imitated from much earlier Chinese blue-and-white porcelain of the first half of the fifteenth century. The next colour to appear was a soft sage-green, a colour derived from iron which tended to burn greyish or brownish olive if the firing was incorrectly gauged. From about 1540 the colour-scheme was expanded to include manganese-purple and up to three subtly differentiated shades of blue, and a soft greenish black was used for the outlines. The painting of these polychrome pieces is much freer, consisting mainly of superb floral designs balanced midway between fantasy and naturalism. A series painted with slight spiral motives has been perversely attributed to potters working in the Golden Horn district of Istanbul,[1] but is technically indistinguishable from the rest of the group. At all stages the drawing has a unique and specifically Turkish quality. The touch is insensitive, indeed scarcely human, and immensely assured. It is as if the designs themselves had dictated to the artist the terms of their own horrifying life.[2]

A detailed study of the designs might well begin with the delicate spiral stems and florets (1), once incorrectly associated with the potteries near the Golden Horn. One piece, a cut-down pear-shaped bottle in the Godman Collection, is an important document in that it bears the Armenian date 978 (=A.D. 1529).[3] It appears to have been ordered by the Armenian community of Kutahya for dedication in a Christian monastery at Ankara—a gift like the ewer made for Abraham of Kutahya in 1510 (2). Blue alone is used for the painting on this bottle and a number of dishes and plates that may also be

[1] First by G. Migeon and A. Sakisian, 'Les faiences d'Asie Mineure,' *Revue de l'art ancien et moderne*, vol. 44, Paris, 1923, pp. 128–9. The Turkish traveller Evliya Celebi described the Istanbul potteries in 1631, and four local varieties of clay; the Istanbul wares were apparently all unglazed drinking-vessels of a kind long popular in the Near East.

[2] A more mechanistic explanation might be that the outlines of the designs were 'pounced' on to the vessels with charcoal dusted through pierced paper cartoons or stencils. A severe discipline in the factories discouraged the painters from showing any individuality in following up with brushwork. Some such process was certainly used for the repeating patterns on tiles, which are 'placed' with unfailing accuracy.

[3] Illustrated by A. Lane, 'The Ottoman Pottery of Isnik,' *Ars Orientalis*, vol. 2, Ann Arbor, 1956, Fig. 33. Round the neck, and in a spiral under the base, are two Armenian inscriptions disguised as ornament, perhaps to escape notice by the Muslim overseers at the factory. One reads: 'Bishop Ter Martiros sent word to Kotays: may the Holy Mother of God intercede for you: send one water-bottle (surahi) here: may Ter Martiros receive it in peace. In the year 978 on the 18th of March this water-bottle was inscribed.' The other reads: 'Ter Martiros sent word from Ankara: may this water-bottle be an object of Kotays for the Monastery of the Holy Mother of God.'

(1) *Plate* 29A; (2) *Plate* 24A.

dated about 1530. The metallic-looking ewer, Plate 29A, has in addition a band of olive-green on the cover. On pieces made nearer the middle of the sixteenth century the spirals are in soft greenish black, with inset arabesque medallions in blue and turquoise. The fine spiral designs, which appear also in the illuminated *tughras* of contemporary imperial edicts, are merely a late version of the coiling foliage that formed the background for inscriptions and figure-designs of so much earlier Islamic art.

A larger group of wares painted in blue and turquoise may be approximately dated between 1525 and 1540 (1). The Isnik potters quite suddenly broke free from the introverted 'Abraham of Kutahya' style, with its metallic shapes and crowded book-illuminators' ornament. They studied the Chinese porcelain that had now become commoner in Turkey; they became aware of Italian maiolica. But in seeking new designs appropriate to pottery they largely drew on their own imagination. Their work has a consequent freshness and originality that recalls the archaic fifteenth-century Italian maiolica rather than any pottery made in the Near East. A dish painted with a snake threatening a bird (2) retains vestiges of the 'Abraham of Kutahya' style, in the buds and leaves that peep round the scalloped edges of the 'contour panel'; and the slight floral wreath round the cavetto looks rather like the 'Golden Horn' spiral patterns. This dish, and another painted with a flower-vase (3), are of shapes taken from Chinese porcelain, and have the expected Chinese lotus-wreath painted round the back. Here for the first time appear the tulips, bluebells, and carnations that were to become such favourite subjects on later Isnik pottery. Stiff, spiky little tulips, often painted in clusters, are almost a hall-mark of the wares made between 1525 and 1550, though in the latest examples they retire into the borders (4); in the second half of the sixteenth century they are still found hiding on the backs of dishes which have more luxuriant blossoms on the front. The Turks had a passion for garden-flowers, especially the tulip, which was first introduced from Turkey into Western Europe by Augier Ghislain de Busbecq, Ambassador of the Emperor Ferdinand I to Istanbul in 1554.[1] The snake's-head fritillary, which also became a European favourite, is seen on a long-necked bottle (5) with the closed crescent— the latter an ancient Turkish motive which since the early Middle

---

[1] Turks who offered him flowers near Adrianople compared their shape to a turban (*tulband*); Busbecq misunderstood this word as the name of the flower itself, and passed it on into European speech. He sent bulbs to Clusius, the famous botanist.

(1) *Plates* 30–2, 33A, 34A; (2) *Plate* 30B; (3) *Plate* 31B.
(4) *Plates* 34B, 37, 38; (5) *Plate* 34A.

LATER ISLAMIC POTTERY

Ages had more commonly appeared in the *chintamani* design, a group
of three crescents with stylized cloud-scrolls. A dish with clusters of
grapes (1) is closely copied from a well-known Chinese type, dating
from the early fifteenth century.[1] Variants of this and other porcelain-
designs are also found painted in polychrome; and there exists a distinct group of wares, probably made in some minor Isnik factory,
where the Chinese designs are somewhat timidly rendered in a poor
blackish blue on vessels potted more thinly than is usual in this period.
A profile medallion portrait of a Turkish youth, with distant hills,
trees and buildings (2), was undoubtedly suggested by similar por-
traits on contemporary Italian maiolica—the source also of the shape,
a dish with wide flat rim and a shallow recess. Also of Italian derivation is the wide-rimmed *tondino* dish with a deep, narrow well (3).
Since the time of Mehmed II the Conqueror the Ottoman Sultans had
shown a healthy respect for Italian art. Costanzo da Ferrara worked at
Istanbul as a medallist, and perhaps as a painter, between 1478 and
1481; Gentile Bellini spent a year there in 1480–1. The great Michel-
angelo himself twice declined invitations to Istanbul; in 1506 he was
to build a bridge over the Golden Horn; in 1519 to paint for Sultan
Selim I.

During their 'blue-and-turquoise' phase of about 1525–40 the
Isnik potters made more tiles than before (4). These were mostly
hexagonal, with neat self-contained patterns of radiating arabesques,
cloud-scrolls, and feathery leaves on interlaced stems. Similar designs
were painted on rectangular tiles that formed a frieze round areas
filled with the hexagons. The colouring is most attractive, with its
bright warm blue and small touches of vivid turquoise—quite different in effect from the more carelessly painted rectangular blue-and-
turquoise tiles of the seventeenth century. In the Topkapu Serai
Palace at Istanbul are a number of huge blue-and-turquoise tile-slabs,
each about five feet high; they have wonderful painting of birds and
Chinese monsters among fantastic foliage.[2] These fine designs are in
a mature Persian-Chinese *hatāyī* style, and must surely have been
supplied to the potters by artists working at the Ottoman court. We
know from the guild registers of 1525–6 that there were then twenty-
nine of these artists, working under the Persian designer Shāh Kulī
of Tabrīz: some had at least twelve years' service. In 1557–8 there

[1] Sir Harry Garner, *Oriental Blue and White*, London, 1954, Plate 14.
[2] K. Otto-Dorn, *Das islamische Iznik*, Berlin, 1941, Plate 47. Celal Esad Arseven, *Les arts décoratifs turcs*, Istanbul, 1952, Fig. 276. E. Akurgal, C. Mango,
R. Ettinghausen, *Treasures of Turkey*, Geneva, 1966, plate on p. 186.

(1) *Plate* 32B; (2) *Plate* 31A.
(3) *Plate* 30A. (4) *Plate* 33A.

were twenty-six court painters divided in groups of Turks and Persians. Enough drawings and manuscripts survive to show that the Persian style of painting had been competently practised at Istanbul since the end of the fifteenth century,[1] and in the splendid reign of Suleyman the Magnificent (1520–66) it was natural that this talent should be pressed into service of all the decorative arts. Its influence became evident in Isnik pottery after about 1540 and culminated in the superb tilework of the second half of the sixteenth century. A few blue-and-turquoise tiles show the new trend, notably a design of two ducks among flowering foliage. There are hexagonal tiles painted in polychrome in the Yeni Kaplica baths at Bursa, which were restored by Rustem Pasha, Suleyman the Magnificent's Grand Vizier and son-in-law. The same polychrome colours of the second Isnik style are also used in a very few examples where the huge patterns run continuously over adjacent rectangular tiles. But until about 1555 the Isnik potters were mainly concerned with vessels, not tiles. After that date, as we shall see, the whole character of the industry changed; tilework became all-important, and vessels took second place.

The vessels painted in polychrome between about 1540 and 1555 are the finest ever made at Isnik (1). It scarcely seems relevant to consider them as works of art; they exist with the conviction of Nature herself, in a mood of excess. It must be Turkish taste that makes the plant-forms look so overwhelming in their narrow space, as if they had grown larger than life, for the contemporary Ottoman textile-patterns have the same blatant character. In the big bowl in the Godman Collection (2) the purple tulips with their sage-green leaves and the long stems of blue flowers appear to spring naturally from the soil of a luxuriant garden; but the floating panels of black and turquoise arabesques are pure fantasy. Elsewhere, chimerical blossoms are brought nearer to the probable by their appearance of growth from a single root (3). Certain mannerisms recur—the wavy 'clip' which binds the flower-stems (it is an adapted Chinese cloud-scroll); the veining scratched through the colour on the leaves or petals; and the panels or bands of tight black arabesques under a turquoise wash.[2] The last seem to have been in fashion for only a short while about the

---

[1] A Sakisian, 'Turkish miniatures,' *Burlington Magazine*, vol. 87, London, 1945, pp. 224–32. C. J. Lamm, 'Miniatures from the Reign of Bayezid II in a Manuscript belonging to Uppsala University Library,' *Orientalia Suecana*, vol. I, 1953, pp. 95–114.

[2] Ogee panels inside the bowl, Plate 37; triangular panels on the mosque-lamp of 1549, Plate 38; band round the lip of the later mosque-lamp, Plate 39.

---

(1) *Plates* 34B, 35–7, *Colour Plates C and D*; (2) *Plate* 37.
(3) *Colour Plate C.*

middle of the sixteenth century. They are found on a mosque-lamp whose rather more conservative decoration is in a restricted colour-scheme of blue, dull turquoise and black (1). This piece is an important document because of the fragmentary inscription round the foot: '. . . thou Holy Man who art at Isnik, Eshref Zade. In the year 956 [=A.D. 1549] on the fifth of the month Jumada. The painter is the poor, the humble Musli' (or 'Mustafa'). It is the only known piece of Isnik pottery that actually bears the name of the place where it was made, included in an invocation to the local saint. The lamp belonged to a set[1] made to the order of Suleyman the Magnificent for the Dome of the Rock in Jerusalem, which he restored in the years after 1545.

Isnik Pottery III: the 'Rhodian' style. About 1555–1700

Indirectly, the work at the Dome of the Rock led to far-reaching changes in the Isnik potteries. The venerable shrine had been built by the Caliph Abd el-Malik in A.D. 691, on the sacred spot from which Muhammad departed on his journey to Heaven. By the sixteenth century the ancient mosaics covering the external walls were in a ruinous state, and Suleyman the Magnificent undertook the pious duty of replacing them with glazed tiles. The task was far beyond the resources of native potters in Syria or Turkey at that time. Isnik had so far made very few tiles, and in Istanbul the *cuerda seca* technique was obsolescent. It would have been natural for Suleyman to look to Persia, where tile-mosaic and *cuerda seca* were competently practised on a very large scale; and in particular to Tabrīz, which he himself visited in military campaigns of 1534 and 1548–9. A painted tile over the north porch of the Dome of the Rock, dated 959 H/1552 A.D., significantly bears the name of the painter Abdullah of Tabrīz. The Persians began work at the highest point of the drum beneath the dome, where there is an inscription in tile-mosaic containing the date 952 H/1545–6 A.D. Below this, mainly on the drum, are *cuerda seca* tiles, and an intermediate type in which the glaze overflows the *cuerda seca* outlines.[2] It appears that in the course of the job the tile-makers worked out for themselves a technique of underglaze painting which is used for most of the tiles. These were made locally, and are of types peculiar to the Dome of the Rock which are not found else-

---

[1] Another, with the neck cut down, is in the Godman Collection. Both were made without bottoms so that the light could shine downwards. See C. D. E. Fortnum, 'On a lamp of Persian ware made for the Mosque of Omar at Jerusalem in 1549,' *Archaeologia*, vol. 42, London, 1869, pp. 387 ff.

[2] I owe these observations to Mr. A. H. Megaw, who kindly allowed me to study the valuable unpublished Report on the Dome of the Rock which he prepared in 1945–6 for the Arab Committee for restoration.

(1) *Plate* 38.

*D. Turkish (Isnik); about 1550. Ht. 12¾ in.
British Museum. (page 53)*

where. The work continued over many years, and in the latest stages made use of tiles imported from the reorganized Isnik factories.

The idea of extensively using underglaze-painted tiles was born; and it was evidently taken to heart by Suleyman's architects, for they introduced more and more tiles into the interior decorations of the splendid mosques built in Istanbul during the second half of the sixteenth century. The series begins with the great Mosque of Suleyman himself, built to designs by the architect Mi'mar Sinān between 1550 and 1557. Here the tilework is confined to the wall above the *mihrāb* and the framing of the windows. The painting is in blue and pale turquoise with black outlines and touches of a new colour—red. In the smaller Mosque of Rustem Pasha (1561) almost the entire inner walls and columns are faced with tiles, as are the walls of the colonnade outside; here the new red is abundantly used, but is still too thinly applied to most of the tiles to be fully effective.[1] In the equally lavish tile-decorations of the Mosque of Mehmed Sokollu Pasha (1571) the red is excellent, the pale turquoise has dropped out, and a deep bluish green (derived from copper) appears in its place.[2] The designs on all these tiles are outlined in an intense black, which is also used to good effect in minor details of the ornament. The tiles themselves are normally square, with sides from $9\frac{1}{2}$ to 13 inches long, and the larger designs with their borders run continuously over a number of adjacent tiles. Some designs are specially shaped to fit the pointed lunettes over windows; on the walls are repeating patterns, or framed compositions in vertical panels some six feet or more in height. The flowering plants, coiling stems with big feathery leaves, cypress-trees, arabesques and inscriptions can thus be planned on a large and imposing scale. As seen on isolated tiles at close quarters, the designs look so aggressive and the colours so exceedingly brilliant that one would expect their massed effect to be overpowering. But this is not so; in the wide, domed interiors of the mosques they create a wonderfully light and airy impression. At a distance it is the flawless white ground that tells most strongly. This tilework, with the associated vessels, is among the most astonishing achievements in the whole range of the potter's art. It defies the ordinary canons of taste, and arouses a sense of disquiet, of *voluptas atque horror*, to see harmony attained by such ruthless means.

To judge from the evidence of dated buildings with contemporary tilework, the standard of colour and drawing remained high throughout the period 1555–1620. The tiles in the galleries of the great

[1] S. P. and H. C. Seherr-Thoss, *op. cit.*, Plates 129–131; E. A. Kurgal, C. Mango, R. Ettinghausen, *op. cit.*, plate on p. 189.
[2] S. P. and H. C. Seherr-Thoss, *op. cit.*, Plate 134.

Mosque of Sultan Ahmed I (the 'Blue Mosque', built 1609–17) are still superb.[1] But thereafter the industry entered a decline through the falling off of orders for new buildings. Decorations in the Baghdad Kiosk (1639) and Circumcision-Room (1641) of the Topkapu Serai appear to have involved the re-use of some huge blue-and-turquoise tiles made about the middle of the previous century.[2] According to the Turkish traveller Evliya Celebi, in 1648 there were only nine potters' workshops at Isnik, compared with three hundred in the time of Ahmed I (1603–17). Tilework executed for the Yeni Valide Mosque between 1663 and 1672 is of inferior quality, the colours being confined to blue and turquoise. Inquiries made in 1718–19 showed that the tile-industry at Isnik was almost extinct, and unable to carry out an Imperial order. The Vizier Daud Ibrahim accordingly rounded up the few remaining skilled craftsmen, and by 1724 had settled them in a new factory in the Tekfur Serai district of Istanbul itself, which was apparently still working in 1773. There are tiles of this revived manufacture in many eighteenth-century buildings in Istanbul, and a tiled fireplace dated 1143 H/1731 A.D. is in the Victoria and Albert Museum. They reproduce old Isnik designs in a rather thin and niggling manner, but the colours, including the red, are still remarkably good. An opaque yellow sometimes found on the Tekfur Serai tiles was never used in the earlier work of Isnik.

The colour-scheme of the polychrome 'Damascus-type' wares made between 1540–55 (1) was so beautiful that it might seem hard to explain why it was so suddenly abandoned. But the sage-green (derived from iron) and the manganese-purple were evidently susceptible to discolouration if the firing conditions were not exactly right, and it would thus have been uneconomical to use them in the mass-production of tiles. Moreover, the soft colour-scheme may not have appeared striking enough in wall-decoration. Hence the adoption of the more strident 'Rhodian' colour-scheme dominated by the new red and the deep copper-green. The pottery vessels made from about 1555 onwards (2) must be regarded as a by-product of the tile-industry. Their designs, however satisfactory, are only excerpts from the larger and far more magnificent compositions on the tiles. A key piece for the introduction of the new colour-scheme is a damaged lamp (3) which came from the Mosque of Suleyman in Istanbul (completed 1557) and must have been made at that time. It has round the neck a narrow band of black-and-turquoise arabesques (a feature

[1] *Ibid.*, Plates 136, 137.   [2] See p. 52.

(1) *Plates* 34B, 35–7, *Colour Plate C*; (2) *Plates* 39–47.
(3) *Plate* 39.

shared with slightly earlier pieces in a different colour-scheme (1));
there is a good deal of purplish black, the usual blue, and a mottled,
brownish tomato-red. This last colour is too thinly applied to attain
the brilliance seen in pieces of a slightly later date. There are a few
dishes (2) and tankards on which the same brownish red is used in
conjunction with the sage-green, purple and soft blues of the 'Damascus' type. The effect is not happy, and the rarity of such pieces
suggests that the 'transitional' phase they represent lasted only a very
short time.

The red at its best is a true scarlet, and is applied so thickly as to
stand up in perceptible relief from the surface. It has been aptly
compared to sealing-wax. It is in fact a 'slip' of the highly ferruginous
clay which was known to medieval and renaissance Europe as 'Armenian bole' and valued for its medicinal properties as an astringent. The
best bole came, as its name implies, from Turkish territory; but
according to the potter Bernard Palissy there were also deposits in
France. Palissy did not regard it as a potter's colour. But Italian
potters were attempting to use it as such on their maiolica at the very
time when it first appeared at Isnik.[1] A good red that can be fired
under the glaze has always been a difficult colour for potters to master,
whether in Italy or the Near East; the infusible ferruginous clay is apt
to repel the glaze and emerge with a dull, rough surface. The Isnik
potters probably owed their remarkable success to their exceptionally
viscous and stable glaze, which adhered perfectly as a glassy film over
the raised red areas.

Among the Isnik pottery vessels made after 1555 (3) the commonest
shape is the flat-rimmed dish derived from Chinese porcelain. Early
examples almost invariably have the Chinese wavy edge and the
painted 'wave-and-rock' border (4). Towards 1600 the edges became
plain circles, the wavy pointed lobes being indicated only by painted
lines enclosing the border-pattern. On seventeenth-century dishes
these lines too become plain concentric circles (5), and the waves set
into meaningless clusters of spirals with S-shaped punctuations. They
have sometimes been nicknamed 'ammonite scrolls' by writers who
did not understand their derivation. Another favourite shape is the
platter with a narrow flat rim (6). The Italianate wide-rimmed dish

---

[1] Cipriano Piccolpasso, *Li tre libri dell' arte del vasaio*, transl. and ed. B.
Rackham and A. van de Put, Victoria and Albert Museum, London, 1934, pp. 39,
51, 64. Piccolpasso was writing between 1556–9. He seems unaware that this red
had been used for half a century past by potters at Faenza, Siena and Cafaggiolo.

---

(1) Plates 37, 38; (2) *Plate* 40B; (3) *Plates* 39–47; (4) *Plates* 40B, 41B.
(5) *Plates* 46B, 47A; (6) *Plates* 42B, 43B.

with a shallow recess does not long survive (1). The characteristic tankard or jug is pear-shaped (2), the neck not being offset from the body as in earlier Isnik tankards. A cylindrical mug (3) which was used as a flower-vase has a curiously-cut flat handle which betrays its derivation from a vessel made of bound wooden slats. A covered bowl (4) and a bottle with a knop in the long neck are old shapes; new are the pierced flower or pot-pourri vases (5) and a dish made in one piece with the high spreading foot. A spherical object with a hole pierced for suspension at the top and painting on its lower part was intended to hang as decoration in a mosque;[1] this shape had already appeared at Isnik in the early sixteenth-century 'Abraham of Kutahya' phase, and is perpetuated in the 'Easter eggs' made at Kutahya by Armenian potters in the eighteenth century. It is not found in other Near Eastern countries.

The most characteristic designs are those which show growing plants—carnations, tulips, roses, bluebells and cypress-trees, combined with the long serrated leaves known to the Turkish decorators as *saz* (6). There are, needless to say, many arabesque-forms, and some of the most effective pieces are those in which the designs are deliberately simplified as a means of contrasting colours (7). In a small and rare group the painting is in coloured slips on a ground coloured salmon-pink, deep chocolate-brown, or pale blue (8). Queer animals occasionally appeared in Isnik decoration as early as about 1530, and continued in later times (9); they are so naïvely drawn as to seem the unaided creations of the pot-painters. The same is true of the human figures; the Turkish youth and girl in Plate 43A must date from the sixteenth century, but almost all the others appear to have been painted about 1640 or later. The designs of ships (10), three-master or lateen-rigged, also date mostly from the seventeenth century. The vessels made between about 1620 and 1700 can be recognized by their poor drawing and inferior colours; the red especially has a brownish tone, and the blue and green run badly in the glaze.

In its own day the Isnik pottery had a high reputation in Europe. It was sold by numerous retailers in Istanbul, where the Venetian and

---

[1] Sometimes incorrectly regarded as weights to counterbalance the hanging mosque-lamps. In the Yeni Valide Mosque at Istanbul several seventeenth-century Chinese blue-and-white porcelain vases hang as ornaments at the end of long chains.

---

(1) *Plate* 42A; (2) *Plate* 44A, *Colour Plate F. Compare Plate* 32A.
(3) *Plates* 45A, 46A; (4) *Colour Plate E.*
(5) *Plate* 41A; (6) *Plate* 41; (7) *Plate* 46A, *Colour Plate F.*
(8) *Plate* 44, 45A; (9) *Plate* 42A; (10) *Plate* 46B.

Genoese merchants had headquarters, and through Venice found its way into Germany and the north. We learn from the Journal of Stephen Gerlach, secretary of the Austrian Embassy to the Sublime Porte between 1573 and 1578, that his master, David Ungnad, had spent over 100 ducats on pottery vessels and 1000 thalers on 'Nicaean tiles' for shipment via Venice.[1] In the Museum at Halle is a silver-gilt cover and mount, evidently made for an Isnik pottery tankard now broken and lost. It bears the inscription:

> *Zu Nicea bin ich gemacht*
> *Und nun gen Halle in Sachsen bracht*
> *Anno* 1582.

('I was made at Isnik, and now brought to Halle in Saxony, in the year 1582');[2] the engraved armorials are those of Johann Friedrich, later Elector of Brandenburg, who lived at Halle between 1566 and 1598 and had served in the Turkish wars. Three jugs or tankards have English silver-gilt mounts made by the London silversmith 'I.H.' between 1586 and 1598.[3] Thomas Platter, a Swiss who visited England in 1599, reports seeing 'a Turkish pitcher and dishes' in the curiosity-cabinet of Mr. Cope, 'a citizen of London who has spent much time in the Indies'; and according to an inventory of 1612 the Mouth Tavern without Bishopsgate had in its kitchen 'one earthen Turkey bason, with painted dishes' valued at one shilling and sixpence.[4] A service of large and small Isnik dishes of unusual shape bears amid the floral designs a shield of arms, apparently that of the European family for whom it was made.[5] And a number of pierced flower-vases bear under

---

[1] *Stephan Gerlach des Älteren Tagebuch*, Frankfurt am Mayn, 1674, p. 380.

[2] M. Sauerlandt, *Edelmetallfassungen in der Keramik*, Berlin, 1929, p. 43. F. Sarre, 'Die Fayencen von Nicaea und ihr Export nach dem Abendland,' *Pantheon*, vol. 24, 1939, p. 341.

[3] (1) Former Swaythling Collection, 1586–7. (2) Fitzwilliam Museum, Cambridge, former Dysart Collection, 1592. (3) British Museum, Franks Collection, 1597–8, all illustrated in *Burlington Fine Arts Club, Exhibition of the Faience of Persia and the Nearer East*, London, 1908, Plate 22. A fourth, in the Victoria and Albert Museum, has undated mounts by the same maker; these have hitherto been described as Utrecht work of about 1580 owing to a misinterpretation of a casting-mark (information kindly supplied by my colleague, Charles Oman).

[4] *Thomas Platter's travels in England*, ed. C. Williams, London, 1937, p. 73. *Illustrations of the manners and expences of antique times in England, in the fifteenth, sixteenth and seventeenth centuries, deduced from the accompts of Churchwardens, and other authentic documents*, London, 1797, p. 232. (I owe these two references to my colleague Robert Charleston.) Isnik dishes may well have suggested the tulip designs on English delftware 'blue-dash-chargers' and their Dutch kindred. An Isnik dish has now been excavated in England, at Waltham Abbey: see P. J. Huggins, 'Excavations at Sewardstone Street, Waltham Abbey, Essex, 1966', *Post-Medieval Archaeology*, vol. 3, 1969, pp. 70, 87, 93, Plate 1.

[5] Plate 45B, arms not identified, but probably not Mocenigo of Venice, as has been sometimes stated.

the base a mark in black of a long-stemmed cross intersected by a capital letter 'S' (I); this resembles the marks on Italian maiolica drug-jars, and suggests that the vases were made to order for Italy. A continuous importation of Isnik pottery throughout the seventeenth century is suggested by the close imitations in maiolica made at Padua.[1] Indeed it would seem that when Turkish orders for tiles fell off the Isnik potters came to rely on their European and Greek customers. A great number of rather poorly-painted dishes were preserved until the nineteenth century in the stone-built Greek houses at Lindos in the Island of Rhodes. Over five hundred of these were acquired for the Cluny Museum, whose catalogue of 1883 first gave currency to the fantastic idea that they were made in Rhodes by descendants of the Crusaders.[2] It will probably never be possible to stop dealers and collectors calling the later Isnik wares 'Rhodian', and the nickname is at any rate a convenient label for the whole class in which the 'sealing-wax red' appears. A number of dishes with dates between 1646 and 1669 bear phonetically spelt Greek inscriptions in the border, round designs of pagoda-like buildings or poorly-drawn figures (2). The date 1678 and other Greek inscriptions appear on tiles still *in situ* in the Katholikon church of the Megiste Lavra monastery on Mount Athos, to which they were given by the Patriarch Dionysos of Constantinople, who ended his days there. Thereafter Isnik pottery fades into obscurity. No vessels have as yet been attributed to the tile-factory established in 1724 in the Tekfur Serai district of Istanbul.[3]

Later imitations of Isnik pottery

In the nineteenth century and later the old Isnik designs have been adapted by the Armenian potters of Kutahya for use on vessels of curious shape and rather poor technique; the usual 'Rhodian' colour-scheme is often supplemented by an opaque pale yellow. In 1898 a Persian potter in Isfahan was supplied with drawings of 'Damascus-

[1] These imitations, once wrongly attributed to Candiana, bear dates from 1601 to 1697. A yellow-brown serves as substitute for the Isnik red. See A. Moschetti, 'Delle maioliche dette "Candiane",' in *Bollettino del Museo Civico di Padova*, vol. 7, 1931, pp. 1–58. B. Rackham, *Catalogue of Italian Maiolica*, Victoria and Albert Museum, London, 1940, p. 139. L. Conton, *Le antiche ceramiche veneziane scoperte nella Laguna*, Venice, 1940, pp. 93, 119.

[2] E. du Sommerard, *Catalogue et description des objets d'art*, Musée des Thermes et de l'Hôtel de Cluny, Paris, 1883, pp. 178–93. The idea was already refuted by O. von Falke, *Majolika*, Berlin, 1907, pp. 44–5. The Cluny dishes are now scattered through various French public collections. There are still many pieces in the delightful houses at Lindos.

[3] See p. 56.

(I) *Plate* 41A, *p.* 114; *No.* 14; (2) *Plate* 47B.

E. *Turkish* (*Isnik*)*; about* 1560–80. *Ht.* $9\frac{1}{4}$ *in.*
British Museum. (*page* 57)

type' dishes in the Godman Collection, and made to order a series of unmarked imitations which may still be current in the antique market. They are thickly potted in a light and brittle buff material, with a white slip and a slightly crackled transparent glaze which lies unevenly over the painting; the drawing is rather lifeless, with purple-black outlines and too-pale colours, except for the harsh bright blue. After the First World War potters were brought from Kutahya to Jerusalem to begin the formidable task of repairing Suleyman the Magnificent's tilework on the Dome of the Rock. They made few tiles (the Dome still awaits repair), but cater for tourists with wares in a debased Isnik style. In Europe, the earliest modern imitations of Isnik ware were made between 1861 and 1887 by Théodore Deck of Paris; they usually bear his signature. Deck was a very intelligent man who really understood the fundamentals of Near Eastern technique.[1] His imitations of the 'Damascus' and 'Rhodian' types are very good, being made of materials akin to those of the originals, but his glaze was inclined to crackle. Similar French imitations were made at Chatillon-sur-Seine by E. Lachenal, in the 1880's; and at Choisy-le-Roi by Léon Parvillée, who restored the tilework of the Green Mosque at Bursa. Deck's exhibits at the Paris Exhibition of 1861 probably inspired those made by Minton and Co. of Stoke-on-Trent for the International Exhibition of 1862. These are of a very white translucent porcelain, painted in unpleasantly hard colours; they are unmarked. William De Morgan, working successively in Chelsea, Merton Abbey (from 1882) and Fulham (from 1888–1907), borrowed inspiration in colour and design from the 'Damascus-type' wares for his art pottery and tiles; the same influence is apparent in much of the other decorative art produced by De Morgan's friend William Morris. But De Morgan did not make close imitations and his material was a rather flimsy white earthenware. From 1878 onwards Cantagalli of Florence has made imitations of the 'Damascus' and 'Rhodian' types in maiolica—a hard, brownish-buff earthenware coated with white tin-glaze, and with a glossy transparent lead-glaze laid over the painting. The colours are often rendered with such uncanny skill that they might deceive, were it not for the difference in material and the factory-mark of a sketchily-painted cockerel. More recently some poor imitations have been made in Athens and some better ones in the Island of Rhodes. There are also some dangerous forgeries, probably made by Samson of Paris, of the blue-and-white 'Abraham of Kutahya' pieces; their material is hard and metallic, almost like porcelain. Samson has made imitations of 'Rhodian' with quite good colours but unconvincing shapes.

[1] In his book *La faïence*, Paris, 1887, pp. 245–58, Deck gives an illuminating account of the materials and colours he used.

61

LATER ISLAMIC POTTERY

Syrian pottery of the Ottoman period. About 1560–1700

By the time of the Ottoman conquest in 1516 the once-thriving potteries of Damascus[1] appear to have sunk into obscurity. We have already considered the restorations in tilework at the Dome of the Rock in Jerusalem, begun under Suleyman the Magnificent in 1545; their influence in reorientating the Isnik factories towards tilework; and the first considerable use of these tiles in the Mosque of Suleyman in Istanbul, built between 1550 and 1557.[2] The work at the Dome of the Rock appears to have stimulated a similar movement in Syria. For between 1554 and 1560 Suleyman built another important mosque, in Damascus; and here, in the tympana over the windows and doors of the great court, are the first of another notable series of painted tiles.[3] The designs are of the Persian-Chinese character that had become international, and their broad handling, with stiff black outlines, suggests that they were immediately derived from tilework in the *cuerda seca* technique. It is indeed probable that Persians trained in that tradition had moved to Damascus after completing their task at the Dome of the Rock. Later buildings in Damascus, particularly the Mosque of Sinān (1585), have tiles which show the development of more detailed freehand brushwork; there is a preference for such motives as cypress-trees, flower-vases, and wavy vine-branches. At this time the tile-makers of Damascus and Isnik were apparently pursuing quite distinct, though parallel, courses. But it is just possible that the colour-scheme of the Damascus tiles had been suggested by earlier imports from Isnik, not of tiles, but of pottery vessels. For there are a few fine bowls, undoubtedly made at Damascus, which seem to be imitated from Isnik wares of the so-called 'Damascus' group (1). The colours are cobalt-blue, turquoise, purple, black outlines, and a green ranging from pale apple-green to a muddy olive. To this colour-scheme the Damascus potters remained faithful both in their tiles and in a series of pottery vessels whose shapes and painted designs betray familiarity with the Isnik wares painted in the 'Rhodian' colours of the second half of the sixteenth century (2). The Damascus wares are technically inferior to those of Isnik; like all Syrian pottery, they have a glassy crackled glaze, a dirty yellowish-white ground, and careless drawing in colours that tend to run. The material is softer than that of Isnik, and more roughly finished at the foot-ring; dishes usually have three conspicuous spur-marks inside.

[1] Pp. 15–18, 29–30.   [2] Pp. 54–5.
[3] Arthur Lane, 'The Ottoman pottery of Isnik,' *Ars Orientalis*, vol. 2, Ann Arbor, 1956, Fig. 48.

(1) *Plate* 48B; (2) *Plate* 48A.

Needless to say, the 'sealing-wax-red' of Isnik never appears. The designs are not mapped out with the unfailing exactness of Isnik; they seem rather to be dashed in spontaneously by the painter, whose touch shows a certain spirit in the outlines. The manufacture of these vessels and tiles probably continued throughout the seventeenth century.

The Armenian potters of Kutahya: mainly eighteenth century

The ancient Armenia, the region south of the Caucasus round Mount Ararat and Lake Van, is now divided between Turkey, Russia and Persia. Its inhabitants were converted to Christianity by St. Gregory the Illuminator in the second half of the third century A.D. The wars of the Middle Ages dispersed the Armenians from what was a natural frontier province, and all over Asia Minor they settled in communities where at times they were able to maintain their independence. Their technical and professional skill is still evident in the Near East today, and during the sixteenth century some of them worked as employees in the potteries of Isnik.[1]

At Kutahya, about seventy-five miles south from Isnik, the Armenian colony ran potteries of its own. These are first heard of in 1608, when the Turkish governor received instruction from Istanbul that the 'masters who make cups in Kutahya' should sell some of their soda (a raw material for pottery) at current prices to the potters of Isnik, who had run short in completing an Imperial order for tiles. In 1669–1670 Evliya Celebi wrote of his visit: 'Kutahya has thirty-four quarters, among them the quarter of the infidel china-makers . . . their dishes and cups, their various drinking-vessels and jugs, their bowls and plates are not only for local consumption. But the dishes of Isnik are more world-famous.' In 1700 'Kutahya cups' were dutiable articles at Tokat; and in 1710 the Kutahya potters received an Imperial order from Istanbul for 9500 tiles, including 1000 large and 1500 small 'with inscriptions'.[2] (It is not known whether the tiles were delivered; presumably they had proved unobtainable from the failing factories at Isnik.) In 1715 the French merchant Paul Lucas sent from Istanbul *'une douzaine de tasses à café avec leurs soucoupes, une tasse, deux bouteilles pour mettre de l'eau de rose, deux salières et deux escritoires, le tout de porcelaine de Cutajé'*. It has not been possible to identify any existing Kutahya pottery of the seventeenth century, with the possible exception of some rather heavy barrel-shaped mugs;[3] but the

[1] Pp. 44, 50.

[2] References quoted from R. Anhegger, in K. Otto-Dorn, *Das islamische Iznik*, Berlin, 1941, pp. 148, 171, 194, 209.

[3] John Carswell, 'A minor group of late Turkish pottery,' *Sanat Tarihi Araştirmala* I, *Istanbul Universitesi Edebiyat Fakültesi, Sanat Tarihi Enstitüsü*, 1965, pp. 1–15, discusses these and related vessels and prefers to date them to the second half of the eighteenth century.

descriptions given by Lucas would apply exactly to known examples of the eighteenth century. The factories specialized in rather slight and trivial wares, with a side-line in tiles for decorating Armenian churches.

The walls of the Armenian cathedral of St. James in Jerusalem are covered with square tiles, mostly with geometric designs in blue-and-white; but among them is a series of thirty-seven very naïvely painted in polychrome with scenes from the Old and New Testaments, Christ, Saints, and Archangels.[1] An Armenian inscription at the top of each names the subject; the inscriptions at the bottom were evidently intended to read continuously from one tile to the next, and name various Armenians of Kutahya who had each contributed a number of tiles for the restoration in the year 1168 (=A.D. 1719) of the Church of the Resurrection in Jerusalem. The original series must have consisted of more than 160 tiles; it failed to reach its destination in the Church of the Resurrection because the Greek Christians had meanwhile secured for themselves the privilege of repairing that building. The tiles are of white material painted in bright opaque yellow, green, blue, purple, and 'sealing-wax-red', with black outlines. The figure-subjects are in what might be euphemistically called a provincial Byzantine style.

A number of vessels painted with Christian subjects bear the same date, corresponding to A.D. 1719, and were no doubt intended for the same destination as the tiles. In the Victoria and Albert Museum is a plate inscribed 'Archangel 1168' (1) with St. Michael receiving a dead man's soul; on the back is written 'Wartabed Abraham'. A dish similarly inscribed and dated, with the decapitation of St. John Baptist, is in the Armenian Church of San Lazaro in Venice. In the Musée d'Art et d'Histoire, Brussels, is a bowl with the twelve Apostles ranged round the inside, and outside three amusing scenes of hunters shooting a bird, soldiers attacking a walled town, and a procession approaching an enthroned prince.[2] An inscription records that it was made for Wartabed Abraham, Bishop of Takirdag (north of the Dardanelles) in 1719. A saucer-dish of 1719 in Brussels, and another formerly in the Kelekian Collection, show equestrian figures of St. Sergius and two 'warrior saints'. An 'incense box' shaped like a squat, lobed tankard, formerly in the Kelekian collection, bears the date 1170

---

[1] Illustrated by Ch. A. Nomikos, *The Christian Pottery-Work of the Armenian Patriarchate in Jerusalem*, Alexandria, 1922 (in Greek); J. Carswell, *Kütahya Tiles*, Oxford, 1971.

[2] Arthur Lane, 'Turkish Peasant Pottery from Chanak and Kutahia,' *Connoisseur*, vol. 104, 1939, pp. 232–7.

---

(1) *Plate* 50A.

($=$A.D. 1727) (1). On an undated plaque in the British Museum is a group showing the fifth-century translators of the Bible, St. Sahik Parthev and St. Mesrop (who also invented the Armenian alphabet); St. Nerses the Poet (*d.* 1165), and St. Gregory of Nerek the Rhetorician. Tiles in the Sèvres Museum painted with Christian subjects bear dates as late as A.D. 1843. To the same category belong the numerous 'Easter eggs', painted with heads of cherubs and pierced at both ends for suspension as ornaments in a church.

The Kutahya tiles are not attractive, with their dingy white ground and dull colours, mainly grey-blue, green and yellow; their repeating plant-designs are nondescript and formless. The 'useful wares', on the other hand, are often very pleasing, especially the domed coffee-pots and the tall cups and saucers whose shape suggests the influence of early Vienna or Meissen porcelain. Shallower cups of the late eighteenth century often have an imitation of the crossed-swords mark found on the Meissen cups which were mass-produced for the Turkish market. Another mark commonly found is the word *Siwaz* in Turkish characters; this cannot be interpreted to mean the town Sivas, and its significance is not known. There are flattened pilgrim-flasks, long-necked sprinklers for rose-water, incense-burners with pierced covers, bowls, and plates, all very finely potted in a translucent material which could well be described as 'peasant-porcelain'. The larger jugs are often very ugly in shape, with ribbing in relief. The painted designs sometimes betray consciousness of Chinese blue-and-white porcelain, but are usually of a simple-minded geometrical or floral character. They make a gay show of colour—bright opaque yellow, emerald-green, blue, purple and red, the last commonly applied in a line of dots round the chief patterns. Very characteristic are the figures of ladies in trousers and high striped caps, and turbaned gentlemen with fierce moustaches (2).[1]

A French traveller, Charles de Peyssonnel, remarked in 1755 a considerable export of Kutahya ware to the Crimea, and it seems to have found its way all round the Levant, where it is still avidly sought by collectors. Samson of Paris has found it worth while to make some rather good imitations, of which only the showroom samples bear his 'oriental' mark.[2] They have a glistening white paste and a poor, pale yellow. From the middle of the nineteenth century until the present day a few potters in Kutahya have continued to make unconvincing imitations of the Isnik 'Rhodian' ware.

[1] Illustrations, R. H. R. Brocklebank, 'Anatolian Faience from Kutiyeh,' *Burlington Magazine*, vol. 60, 1932, p. 246.
[2] Pp. 114, 115.

(1) *Plate* 50B; (2) *Plate* 51D.

LATER ISLAMIC POTTERY

Chanak Kalé pottery: nineteenth century

A good deal of unpretentious but often very attractive peasant pottery was made during the first half of the nineteenth century at Chanak Kalé on the Dardanelles. The best pieces are dishes, jars and bowls of reddish earthenware decorated in purple and in coloured clay slips under a yellowish lead-glaze (1). The broadly drawn designs include ships of the Trafalgar period, garden pavilions with trees, coffee-pots, and simple geometric and plant motives, most often rendered in purple on a white ground with touches of thick yellow-ochre slip. Alternative slip colours are a thick blue, white and tomato-red, and sometimes these are laid on a ground of ochre or putty-coloured slip. These wares have a wide distribution round the Eastern Mediterranean, but little documentation about them exists. Examples presumably new at the time were brought back to the Sèvres Museum between 1830 and 1844.[1] There is a good selection at Istanbul in the Topkapu Serai.

The same potteries continued to make some very ugly braziers and jugs whose long necks terminate with an animal head; these are glazed green or brown, have clumsy applied flowers and stems, and are often painted with flowers in unfired gold or other colours.[2] The Victoria and Albert Museum has examples acquired at Gallipoli in 1862. Also typical are the fairly common vessels in the form of long-legged horses or camels, which pour from the mouth and have holes for filling in the back. These are marbled in brown, white, purple, and green.

Turkish porcelain: nineteenth century

Two distinct factories in Istanbul have made hard-paste porcelain of the French type, but little documentation about them has been published. The first was founded in the second half of the nineteenth century on the Golden Horn, and marked its productions 'Eseri Istanbul' (products of Istanbul) in Arabic characters, impressed. The plates, carafes, covered cups, and bowls were somewhat vulgarly painted with blowsy naturalistic flowers, often with gilt rococo relief-work, in a contemporary European style.[3] This factory closed after

[1] A. Brongniart and D. Riocreux, *Description méthodique du Musée Céramique de la Manufacture Royale de Porcelaine de Sèvres*, Paris, 1845, pp. 156–7, 186. Celal Esad Arseven, *Les arts décoratifs turcs*, Instanbul, 1952, Figs. 425, 428. Arthur Lane, 'Turkish Peasant Pottery of Chanak and Kutahia,' *Connoisseur*, vol. 104, 1939, pp. 232–7.

[2] Celal Esad Arseven, *op. cit.*, Fig. 299.

[3] Celal Esad Arseven, *Les arts décoratifs turcs*, Istanbul, 1952, Figs. 426, 438, 439–41; examples in the Victoria and Albert Museum.

(1) *Plate* 49.

finding itself unable to compete with the wares of similar character which were more cheaply produced in Europe. The second factory was founded by Abdul Hamid II in 1893 in the grounds of the Palace of Yildiz and was active until 1920; its wares, of rather superior quality, were intended almost exclusively for the palace and for diplomatic presents. They are marked with a star and crescent, printed in green.[1]

[1] H. Kocabaş, *Porselencilik Tarihi*, Bursa, 1941, pp. 63–68, 116.

4

PERSIA: THE SAFAVID PERIOD
(1502-1722) AND LATER

Persia set the fourteenth-century 'Mongol' fashions in pottery which spread to Syria and Egypt. We cannot say for certain whether Persian fifteenth-century pottery in the Chinese blue-and-white style was better or worse than that made elsewhere: too little has survived. And there is a similar lacuna in our knowledge for the sixteenth century. To judge from imperfect evidence, contemporary Persia produced nothing to compare in splendour with the sixteenth-century Turkish wares of Isnik. But in the seventeenth century, when the Isnik potteries entered a decline, a revival apparently took place in Persia; and though many of the wares then made were relatively unadventurous adaptations from contemporary Chinese blue-and-white porcelain, there were others in which originality was carried almost to excess.

Politically, the Safavid period was one of the most successful and distinguished in Persian history. The dynasty was founded by Shāh Ismā'īl (ruled 1499–1524). His family, long established at Ardebīl on the approach to the Caucasus, traced its descent from Mūsā Kāzim, the seventh Imām in succession to Muhummad's son-in-law 'Alī. The dissenting Shī'a sect, or partisans of 'Alī, flourished in Persia throughout the middle ages, and in the fourteenth century Sheikh Safī ad-Dīn, an ancestor of Shāh Ismā'īl, won such veneration as a holy man as to confer immense religious authority on the royal house that perpetuated his name. Under the courageous and energetic leadership of Shāh Ismā'īl Persia became a unified Shiite nation which for over two centuries more or less successfully repelled the aggression of its orthodox Sunnite neighbours. In the east, after Shāh Ismā'īl had overthrown their chief Muhammad Shaybānī Khan in 1510, the Uzbegs were held by force of arms beyond the frontier of the River Oxus. In the west, where Ismā'īl had annexed Baghdad and Mosul, the Ottoman Turks were a much more formidable enemy. Sultan Selim the Grim invaded Persia and captured Tabrīz in 1514. This city so often

68

changed hands during the many later Turkish invasions that Shāh Tahmāsp (1524–76) moved his capital further east to Qazvīn. A further move took place under Shāh 'Abbās I 'The Great' (1587–1629), who in 1598 transferred his court southwards to Isfahan, nearer the centre of his realm. The estate bequeathed by the military and administrative genius of Shāh 'Abbās was rich enough to support his descendants in comfortable dissipation for a hundred years.[1] Shame and disaster overtook them in 1722, when a handful of Afghan tribesmen conquered the great Persian Empire. For the rest of the eighteenth century Persia was the prey of contending war-lords, until the Kājār dynasty (1779–1925) established a relatively stable background of fear and corruption for the manoeuvres by rival European nations to bring Persia within their spheres of influence.

It was a natural corollary of Turkish agression that Persia should make common cause with the European countries that were similarly threatened. Between 1464 and 1478 embassies were exchanged, and a military alliance formed, between the Venetian Republic and Uzūn Hasan, chief of the White Sheep Turcoman in Western Persia. Venetian attempts to establish friendly relations with Shāh Ismā'īl in 1505 and with Shāh Tahmāsp in 1570 were less successful. In 1567 a daring Englishman, Anthony Jenkinson, initiated on behalf of the British Muscovy Company a series of trading expeditions to Persia via Russia and the Caspian Sea; but these ceased after 1581. Under Shāh 'Abbās the Great European contacts became more frequent and effective. Sir Anthony Sherley and his brother Robert presented themselves to the Shāh in 1598, and though Anthony's mission to secure European aid for Persia was a failure, Robert apparently helped to reorganize the Persian army and to equip it with cannon. Several embassies passed between Isfahan and Venice, and we hear that in 1609 gifts to the Shāh included nine Venetian paintings.[2] Of particular interest is the shopping-list which Shāh 'Abbās sent with his agents to Venice in 1613; it naturally includes decorated glass and mirrors, but it is a surprise to find 'masks for disguise . . . at any price', and 'bulbs and seeds of beautiful flowers, with a note of the time and manner of planting'.[3] Shāh 'Abbās was particularly anxious to secure export for Persian silk by routes avoiding Turkey, which charged high duties;

[1] 'The later Sefavi sovereigns having divided their existence in about equal proportions between the chase, the harem, and the bottle' (G. N. Curzon, *Persia and the Persian question*, London, 1892, vol. 1, p. 395).

[2] G. Berchet, *La Repubblica di Venezia e la Persia*, Turin, 1865, pp. 208–9; a Nativity, a Madonna, a Saviour, a nude lady donning a shift, a Magdalene clothed, a Magdalene nude, the Queen of Cyprus, a Venetian lady, a lady with long hair or Cassandra.

[3] Berchet, *op. cit.*, p. 65.

hence the favourable reception given by him and his successors to European merchants, and the competition between Portugal, Holland and England for trading stations on the Persian Gulf. Thanks to numerous accounts by western travellers we are fairly well informed about seventeenth-century Persia. Some of these writers have real literary merit—the vivacious Thomas Herbert, who went with an English embassy in 1627, and the civilized and humane Chardin, who was court jeweller to Shāh Sulaymān in 1666–9 and 1673–7, and who was knighted by our King Charles II when his Huguenot beliefs caused him to leave France in 1681.[1] We have the picture of an ostentatious court convivially sunk in drink and debauchery, with dancing-girls much in evidence; to which the veiled sufferers of the harem and the blinded princes of the blood royal provide a sinister background.

Safavid art was, to begin with, a continuation of Timurid art. Bihzād, the most celebrated of all Persian miniature-painters, had worked at Herāt for the last descendant of Timur, Sultān Husayn Mīrzā; Shāh Ismā'īl brought him to Tabrīz, and in 1522 made him director of the royal library. The lyrical beauty of Timurid painting lived on in such books as the British Museum Nizāmī, decorated and signed by several famous artists for Shāh Tahmāsp between 1539–43.[2] The same prince commissioned the wonderful carpet of 1540 from the shrine of Sheikh Safī at Ardebīl, which is now in the Victoria and Albert Museum. A new *chīnī khāneh* (porcelain-room) was added to the same shrine in 1611, with shaped niches to house the famous collection of Chinese porcelain which has already been mentioned.[3] Shāh 'Abbās left fine buildings all over Persia, especially in Isfahan, with its tile-clad mosques, spacious town-planning and gardens, and bridges across the Zendeh Rud. To a new suburb at Julfa he deported an industrious community of Armenian Christians. They and the strangely dressed foreigners who were so well received in Persia inspired a 'European' fashion in art, which commonly took the form of large-scale wall-paintings. A Portuguese traveller saw at Shīrāz in 1617 painted figures of women in European dress; similar work elsewhere was attributed to a Greek named Jules, who had learned his art in Italy.[4] According to Pietro della Valle (1628) Shāh 'Abbās had a

[1] Thomas Herbert, *Some yeares travels into Africa and Asia the Great especially describing the famous empires of Persia*, etc. (three seventeenth-century editions; also ed. Sir William Foster, London, 1928). Jean Baptiste Chardin, *Voyages du Chevalier Chardin en Perse, et autres lieux de l'orient*, ed. L. Langlès, 10 vols., Paris, 1811, and other less complete editions.

[2] *A Survey of Persian Art*, Plates 896–9; Laurence Binyon, *The Poems of Nizami*, London, 1928.

[3] P. 28.

[4] Garcia de Silva y Figueroa, quoted by Laure Morgenstern, 'Mural Painting,' in *A Survey of Persian Art*, London and New York, 1938, pp. 1383 ff.

Flemish painter—perhaps 'John the Dutchman', whose work in a palace at Ashraf was seen by Herbert in 1627. The new decorations at the Ali Qapi in Isfahan moved della Valle to remark 'As they do not paint historical or mythological subjects as we do, all these figures are only men and women, either alone or in company, *in modo lascivo*'. And Herbert: 'Next day Hodge-nazar the Armenian Prince was visited by the Ambassador at his house in Jelphea (Julfa): a Christian he professes himself; but (I must be bold to say) his house was furnished with such beastly pictures, such ugly postures, as are indeed not fit to be remembered.' In the Victoria and Albert Museum and elsewhere are panels of brightly coloured *cuerda seca* tilework with large-scale groups of plump young men and women drinking in a garden;[1] their postures are decent, but the puffy jowls and pear-shaped figures are those appropriate to the Safavid way of life. Equally fulsome are the seventeenth-century miniature-drawings signed by Riżā-i 'Abbāsī, Āqā Riżā, and Mu'īn Musawwir, whose unctuous rhythms would appear obscene even without occasional help from the subject-matter.

The pottery of the Safavid period reflects to some extent the same trends as the other arts. Figures in European dress are seen on painted tiles (1); and certain seventeenth-century vessels of bizarre shape, with glazes that smack of bath-salts and ice-cream, appear to have been conceived as harem goods (2). But for several reasons it is not easy to give a satisfactory account of these wares. In the first place, comparatively few can be assigned to the sixteenth century. There is almost nothing to equate with the beautiful miniature-painting as practised under Shāh Ismā'īl and Shāh Tahmāsp. The so-called 'Kubachi' wares almost alone bridge the gap between the fifteenth and seventeenth centuries. There is reason to believe that the brilliant reign of Shāh 'Abbās the Great (1587–1629) was also distinguished for its pottery; but several dated pieces, very good of their kind, show that a high standard was still maintained in the second half of the century. It is easy to recognize the decadence in pottery that followed the downfall of the Safavid dynasty in 1722. Human figures in Persian and European dress were common enough on the 'Kubachi' wares made round about 1600, but tended thereafter to drop out of the repertory. A small class of monochrome wares is moulded in relief with human and animal figures that recall the drawings of the Riżā-i 'Abbāsī school (3). But the Safavid arabesque and plant-motives, in so far as they are of Near Eastern inspiration, are perfunctorily drawn and lack

---

[1] Arthur Lane, *Guide to the Collection of Tiles*, Victoria and Albert Museum, London, 1939, Plate 9A.

---

(1) *Plate* 56A; (2) *Plates* 92–4; (3) *Plates* 96, 97.

the firm grasp of integrated decorative principle that had been the great strength of Islamic art in its prime. It becomes indeed doubtful whether the term 'Islamic art' continues to have meaning when applied to such work. We have seen that in painting the Safavid court attempted to eke out its flagging invention by importing superficial ideas from Europe. In ceramics a more sustained and pervasive influence was exercised by blue-and-white porcelain and celadon wares from China. It is not clear whether the Chinese continued to make celadon for export during the seventeenth-century. But Chardin wrote about 1670 of *porcelaine verte* then in use at the Persian court;[1] and though he personally gave no credence to the belief that celadon disclosed the presence of poison in food, he recorded that the great dishes were valued as high as four or five hundred crowns apiece because of the beauty of their material. Even if the celadon current in Persia during the seventeenth century was already 'antique', its reputation still encouraged the native potters to reproduce it with many interesting variants of their own. Next to the blue-and-white, the monochrome glazed wares derived from celadon are the most numerous and characteristic productions of the Safavid period.

The shapes of the Safavid wares are in many cases as dependent on Chinese models as their decoration. Herbert observed in 1628 that 'They (the Persians) commonly eat in earth or porcelain, not valuing silver (the King by such attracting it to his own table)'.[2] The big pilaf-dishes, bowls, jars, and bottles often bear very evident signs of use, for rancid butter, a delicacy beloved by the Persians, has penetrated through cracks in the glaze, discolouring the material and stinking with still undiminished power. Broken necks and spouts are often restored in engraved brass of poor workmanship and nineteenth-century date. Among the more peculiar shapes are the water-containers for 'hubble-bubble' tobacco-pipes (*kaliāns*). The simplest are roughly spherical, with a hole at the top through which a tube ran down into the water from the burning tobacco in its metal pan (1). A smaller hole to the side, above water-level, received the long tube leading to the mouth of the smoker, whose inhalations drew the smoke through the water with a *iucundo strepitu*, as Kaempfer quaintly puts it.[3] Other *kaliāns* are directly copied or adapted from vessels of Chinese porcelain which were originally intended for pouring or drinking, and

[1] See Appendix, p. 122.

[2] *Some Yeares Travels*, etc., 3rd ed., p. 328.

[3] Engelbert Kaempfer, *Amoenitatum exoticarum politico-physico medecinarum fasciculi V . . . descriptiones rerum Persicarum*, etc., Lemgoviae, 1712, p. 461.

(1) *Plates* 57A, 74A, 87A.

not for tobacco-smoking (1).[1] Some *kaliāns* are in the forms of birds or animals (2). A curious ewer illustrated in Plate 75A has an almost exact counterpart in Safavid engraved brass;[2] it is filled through an orifice in the hollow handle which, in the metal prototype, has a hinged cap. Similar hollow handles with filling-holes are found on ewers with monochrome glazes, of the class represented in Plates 92–4. These are internally divided into two compartments; the lower one, served by the handle and spout, containing the drink; the upper one holding ice inserted down the wide neck. Chardin gives a most interesting account of the manner in which the Persians worked hard during the winter to bury a large stock of ice for use in the hot months.[3] A metallic-looking bowl with spout of square section (3) is probably descended from a Mongol shape, found also in Chinese fourteenth-century porcelain. Murdoch Smith reported that these bowls were used by ladies to pour water over themselves in the bath, and some colour is given to this statement by the fact that they are seen in the hands of the ladies *en déshabillé* painted on two 'Kubachi' tiles (4). 'Bath-rasps' for scrubbing the body take the form of sitting birds or ladies' slippers, unglazed and cross-grooved on their lower surface. Large knobs attached to flat disks were used to weight carpets spread in the open air. A vase with multiple short nozzles (5) was intended for growing tulips or other bulbs, whose roots trailed down to water inside. This idea passed from Persia to Holland, where the Delft potters of the later seventeenth century adapted it for their huge 'tulip-vases' such as may be seen at Hampton Court.[4]

An attempt at classifying the late Persian wares will be made in subsequent chapters, but here is the place to confess why any classification possible with our present resources is bound to be unsatisfactory. Though some of the classes are well defined in their style and technique, we do not know for certain where any of them were made. The single seventeenth-century piece inscribed with a place-name[5] is

---

[1] Compare Soame Jenyns, *Ming Pottery and Porcelain*, London, 1953, Plate 20A (about 1400); Plates 68A, 100B. His Plate 96A, a 'late Ming export' bottle with a slender tubular spout, is a variant of the same basic form. See also full discussion by J. A. Pope, *Chinese Porcelains from the Ardebil Shrine*, Washington, 1956, pp. 116–18.

[2] Victoria and Albert Museum, no. 457—1876, dated 1011 H/1602–3 A.D.

[3] Ed. Langlès, Paris, 1811, vol. 4, pp. 62–4.

[4] Arthur Lane, 'Daniel Marot: Designer of Delft Vases and of Gardens at Hampton Court,' *Connoisseur*, vol. 123, 1949, p. 19.

[5] The ewer signed by Mahmūd Mi'mār of Yezd, p. 99.

---

(1) *Plates* 79A, 88B; (2) *Plates* 76A, 77A; (3) *Plate* 92B.
(4) *Plate* 56B, C; (5) *Plate* 85A.

not a typical specimen. The troubles of the eighteenth century not only terminated the Safavid traditions of pottery; they blotted out the very existence of the old factories from human memory. When later European travellers and collectors began to be interested, they could obtain little reliable information on the spot about the origin of the pieces they acquired in Persia. An essay of fifty pages on Persian pottery by Comte Julien de Rochechouart[1] is quite remarkably unhelpful. He observed that jars and large dishes with hollow-moulded arabesques under a celadon glaze were in his time universally attributed to Kirmān; the superior blue-and-white wares with black outlines he considered were made at Meshed. He was impressed by the wretched quality of the nineteenth-century wares. The bulk of the very comprehensive collection of Safavid and later Persian pottery in the Victoria and Albert Museum was acquired in Persia in 1874–6 by General Sir Robert Murdoch Smith, with the help of Monsieur Richard, a Frenchman who had lived many years in the country and married a Persian wife. In his booklet on *Persian Art*[2] Murdoch Smith distinguished seven classes of pottery, and his remarks about their local distribution deserve some respect. He attributed the two principal classes of blue-and-white to Yezd and Kāshān. Safavid pottery vessels commonly bear imitation Chinese marks, and in the *Catalogue of the Stieglitz Museum*, St. Petersburg (1899), these marks were used to supplement a more or less conjectural classification of the wares according to locality.[3] Friedrich Sarre published in 1920 a brief but excellent general discussion of the Safavid wares;[4] and Bernard Rackham read a useful paper in 1933.[5] No other modern studies have been of much value, and as yet practically no evidence about local origins has been derived from archaeological excavations in Persia.

We have, however, a certain amount of contemporary evidence from seventeenth-century European travellers. Raphael du Mans (1660)[6] stated that the Persian makers of faience surpassed those of

[1] *Souvenirs d'un voyage en Perse*, Paris, 1867, pp. 274–326, 'Des poteries' (unillustrated). The author's descriptions are so technically inexact that it is not even possible to recognize his nineteenth-century types.

[2] R. Murdoch Smith, *Persian Art* (South Kensington Museum Art Handbook), London, n.d., about 1875. At that time the pre-Safavid wares were almost unknown, as excavations had hardly begun.

[3] A. A. Carbonier, *Catalogue of Objects in Terracotta, Faience and Maiolica*, Museum of the Central School of Industrial Design of Baron Stieglitz, St. Petersburg, 1899 (in Russian, illustrated).

[4] F. Sarre, 'Wechselbeziehungen zwischen ostasiatischer und vorderasiatischer Keramik,' in *Ostasiatische Zeitschrift*, vol. 8, 1919–20, pp. 337–44.

[5] Bernard Rackham, 'Later Persian Pottery,' in *Oriental Ceramic Society Transactions*, vol. 11, London, 1933–4, pp. 73–5.

[6] *Estat de la Perse en* 1660, ed. Schefer, Paris, 1890, p. 196. The passage, with others from Tavernier and Chardin, are here quoted in the Appendix (pp. 119–123).

Nevers, Cosne and Orléans in France in that their wares were white throughout their substance (the French wares having an ordinary earthenware body covered with a white glaze); the best Persian wares, made at Kirmān, were difficult to distinguish from those of China, which, however, withstood heat better. Du Mans added that the blue used by the Persian potters was imported from Venice in the form of glass.[1] Kirmān was the only pottery-centre mentioned by Tavernier, who was there in 1654; he too remarked that the body was white within and without, coming very near porcelain, but less resistant to heat. Chardin was in Persia from 1666–9 and again from 1673–7; in a fuller account of Persian industries he stated that pottery was one of the things they made best; the finest came from Shīrāz, Meshed, Yezd, Kirmān, and a place in Kirmania named Zorend (Zarand). Chardin in turn noted the white body, the translucency, and the similarity to the 'new' rather than the 'old' Chinese porcelain (by 'old' he may have referred to the heavy fourteenth-fifteenth century types of blue-and-white, or even to celadon). He added that the Dutch were said to mix Persian wares among the Chinese which they exported to Europe. This point has received unexpected confirmation from the records of the Dutch East Indies Company which have recently been published by Dr. Volker.[2] From about 1603 the Dutch had built up an immense trade carrying porcelain and other Chinese goods to markets not only in Europe, but also in Japan, the Pacific, India, and the Near East. They had trading-stations at Gamrun (Bender 'Abbās) and Basra on the Persian Gulf, and at Lar, Shīrāz, and Isfahan. But the troubles that followed the fall of the Ming dynasty (1644) brought Dutch trade with China to a standstill in 1659, and supplies of porcelain had to be sought elsewhere. Some was supplied from the new factories in Japan; but from 1652 the Dutch began to order pottery or 'porcelain' from Persia, for shipment to India, Ceylon, and the Far East. This trade was at its height between 1665 and 1682, when it apparently ceased because Chinese wares were again available. 'Kirmān pottery' was specifically mentioned in several shipments between 1675 and 1682. The British East India Company also dealt in Persian pottery; a letter of 1682 from the London Directors to their factors in Persia asked for 'Goods to be provided . . . Earthenware of Carmania (i.e. Kirmān) and Mushatt

[1] This is hard to believe. The excellent cobalt from Qansar near Kāshān supplied the whole of the Near East and was exported to China and Japan. But the enamel colours used in Europe in the eighteenth century, and no doubt earlier, were largely supplied by Venice in the form of coloured glass cakes. Venice obtained its cobalt-ore from Germany.

[2] T. Volker, *Porcelain and the Dutch East India Company*, Leiden, 1954, pp. 113–16.

(Meshed) made in imitation of China ware of all sorts the finest . . . 100 chests'.[1] According to Volker, some Persian ware must have reached Holland in the seventeenth century, for it is mentioned there in inventories of estates (none seems to have survived, perhaps owing to its relative fragility). By the end of the century the technique of the Persian potters was fairly well understood in Europe; thus Dr. Martin Lister, describing his visit to the Saint-Cloud porcelain-factory in 1698, observes: 'I did not expect to have found it in this perfection, but imagined this might have arrived at the *Gomron Ware*; which is, indeed, little else but a total vitrification'.[2] In 1758 J. G. von Justi wrote that one of the easiest ways to make porcelain was that used by the Persians; the materials were clay, white flint, and white glass; and the results looked so like Chinese porcelain that 'the Dutch and English, who bring a great quantity of it to Europe, always sell it under the name of Chinese, and consequently one never hears of Persian in the market. Only it is not nearly so resistant as the Chinese to boiling hot liquids, and that is why Chinese porcelain has acquired a bad reputation in many quarters, being considered inferior to the Saxon'.[3] Von Justi rightly observed that some contemporary European factories were following Persian methods in making their soft-paste porcelain. It is surprising to learn that in his time Persian pottery was still imported, for we should otherwise have assumed that its quality had so far declined from earlier standards as to make it no longer an attractive article of trade.

By the nineteenth century industrialized Europe had so outstripped the Near East, even in the field of pottery, that the Persian markets were flooded with mass-produced white earthenware from Staffordshire. The designs painted on some contemporary Persian blue-and-white might even have been influenced by Staffordshire blue printing. In polychrome, the palette of the Chinese *famille rose* was favoured, with its strong gold-pink and a nasty bright opaque yellow. But here again the Far Eastern influence seems to have been contaminated by the West; there are Persian *famille rose* plates with patterns evidently copied from those on Mason's 'ironstone china'. The

---

[1] India Office, Letter Book VII, f. 40. I owe this reference to my colleague John Irwin.

[2] *A journey to Paris in the year 1698*, by Dr. Martin Lister, London, 1699, p. 139. Gomron (Gombroon) is Bender 'Abbās, the port on the Persian Gulf from which the Dutch traders shipped Persian pottery to Europe and the Far East. Horace Walpole listed among his possessions at Strawberry Hill 'Two basons of the most ancient Gombroon china' (*Letters to Sir Horace Mann*, vol. 4, 1844, p. 378).

[3] Johann Gottlob von Justi, *Vollständige Abhandlungen von den Manufakturen und Fabriken*, Copenhagen, 1758, p. 413. Quoted in full in the Appendix, p. 122.

technical quality of these wares is often deplorable. If a heavy bowl is picked up by the edge, a piece is quite likely to come away in the hand. Some time after 1850 a conscious revivalism inspired some rather better 'art pottery' made at Teheran; this was evidently intended for tourists and for export to Europe by carpet-dealers. Teheran tiles with figures dressed in Safavid style are to this day very commonly found in England.

5

LATE PERSIAN POLYCHROME WARES

As local attributions are so uncertain, it is for the present most convenient to classify the Safavid wares according to the technique of their decoration. It should, however, be made quite clear that some of the various local centres did not confine themselves to a single method. Besides polychrome, they also made blue-and-white and wares with monochrome glazes. The common origin of all the members of a group is immediately apparent when they are examined; it is attested by similarities of shapes and materials, and sometimes also by marks. Generally speaking, the polychrome wares are more 'Persian', less 'Chinese' in the style and motives of their decoration than the blue-and-white.

The so-called 'Kubachi' wares

We have already referred, in the chapter on fifteenth-century blue-and-white, to the numerous plates and bowls of imported Persian pottery that survived until modern times in the houses of the inhabitants of Kubachi, a remote hill-town in the Caucasian province of Daghestan.[1] It would be natural to assume that these vessels were all acquired from a single, and not very distant, part of Persia; and their common origin is confirmed by peculiarities of technique. All are made of a very soft and porous white composition, with a thin, glassy glaze, very apt to crackle. But the series clearly extends over a long period, and embraces several different styles of decoration. An early group painted in black under pale turquoise glaze is shown by inscribed pieces to have been made in the second half of the fifteenth century (1). This colour-scheme evidently continued long in use; some plates have plant-decoration in the same style as the polychrome pieces with figures in early seventeenth-century dress (2). In one small sub-group the glaze is not turquoise, but bright yellowish-green—a colour developed from copper, probably in conjunction with a higher proportion of lead in the glaze (3). The yellow-green glaze is found on

[1] Pp. 54–6.

(1) *Plate* 20; (2) *Plate* 52B; (3) *Plate* 52A.

78

heavy dishes with the wide foot-ring and wavy rim characteristic of Chinese fourteenth- and early fifteenth-century blue-and-white. The drawing is coarse, and the designs rather nondescript.[1] These pieces probably date from the first half of the sixteenth century, being contemporary with the Isnik imitations of the same heavy Chinese dishes.[2]

The 'Kubachi' blue-and-white forms a parallel series with the black-and-turquoise (I). Here too the heavy, early Ming type of dish prevails in the first half of the sixteenth century, towards the end of which a lighter dish came into fashion, with a wide flat rim and a narrow foot-ring, and decoration derived from Chinese porcelain of the reign of Wan Li (1573–1619). The generally Chinese manner of 'Kubachi' blue-and-white is sometimes modified by inset borders or panels in solid black, through which spirals are incised. Similar black borders appear on a series of early 'Kubachi' polychrome tiles. There exist a few 'Kubachi' pieces with rather poor painting in greenish black alone, under a colourless glaze.

We cannot exactly determine the date when polychrome painting first appears on the 'Kubachi' wares. The earliest examples are not typical, and come from excavations in Persia, not from Kubachi itself. On the dish in Plate 53B, which has a narrow foot, the figures are outlined in black; details are washed in with deep warm blue, pale turquoise, blackish purple, and a thin yellow ochre. The male figure wears a turban bound round a long projecting rod, with a plume beside it—a fashion shown by miniature-paintings to have been current during the first half of the reign of Shāh Tahmāsp (1524–76). The dress and willowy figure of the castanet-dancer, so different from those of later 'Kubachi' ladies, again recall the Shāh Tahmāsp miniatures, and make us regret that the miniaturists did not communicate a greater measure of their delightful art to the potters of this time. This dish and others like it[3] should probably date from about the middle of the sixteenth century. In spite of the unusual colouring, the crackled glaze, the body material, and the leaf and cell-pattern borders are so akin to those of later 'Kubachi' pieces as to leave no doubt that the dish belongs to the same general class.

Some time after 1550 the more typical 'Kubachi' polychrome

---

[1] Other examples illustrated, *Catalogue, T. B. Whitney*, Paris, 1910, no. 89; *The Dikran K. Kelekian Collection of Persian and Analogous Potteries*, Paris, 1910, Plate 83.

[2] See p. 51 and Plate 32B.

[3] *A Survey of Persian Art*, Plate 791C, a dish with a castanet-dancer and a lady in a tree. Another dish, *op. cit.*, Plate 792A, is a forgery.

(I) *Plate* 20.

palette came into use; black outlines; a warm deep blue, inclined to run; clear turquoise; a dirty dull green; a thick opaque yellow-ochre; and a thick brownish red—the last a characteristic colour related to the Isnik 'Armenian bole' but far less brilliant. Very occasionally the yellow-ochre and the red, toned to salmon-pink by the admixture of white slip, are spread over the whole surface as a ground for the super-imposed painting.[1] It might appear possible that the 'Kubachi' colours were adopted in emulation of the polychrome Isnik 'Rhodian' wares which were made after 1550, for a factory in north-west Persia would be readily exposed to Turkish influence, if only through invasion; but the casual, freehand 'Kubachi' drawings, no less than the choice of designs, are completely independent of Turkish models and could hardly be more different in spirit (1). In fact the ware embodies the artistic ideas current in the reign of Shāh 'Abbās the Great (1589–1628). About the time of his death the whole Kubachi series appears to have come to an end. To judge by its decadent style, the only dated piece we have must have been one of the last to be made. This is a tomb-slab in the Victoria and Albert Museum, brought back from Persia by Murdoch Smith, with a bold black inscription com-memorating Mahdi Kuli ibn Ghulam 'Ali Baftabadi, who died in 1037 H/1627 A.D.[2] It has blue cell-pattern borders, and very poor poly-chrome flowers and a mask in the lunette at the top.

Some of the best Kubachi painting is on tiles. The earliest of these are a series represented in the Victoria and Albert Museum,[3] of hexagonal shape with black spiral-incised borders and sketchily drawn animals, birds, and an angel. Two very pleasing rectangular tiles in the same Museum (2), which may have come from a Safavid palace, show dancing-girls prepared for the bath. One lady is salmon-pink, the other white against a salmon-pink ground; both have henna-red hands, and are fortified by corsets against the corpulence which the seventeenth century will bring. There is still a lyrical echo from the sixteenth-century miniature-painting in the background of singing birds and trees in blossom. Among the more typical bust-portraits on the square tiles are some ladies wearing the ruff and tight curls fashionable in Europe about 1600 (3).

[1] Plate 56c (pink); a dish with yellow-ochre ground is illustrated in *Catalogue des anciennes faïences persanes, Damas, Rhodes et Koubatcha composant la collection T. B. Whitney*, Paris, 1910, no. 96. The fine Whitney Collection is now in the Musée des Arts Décoratifs, Paris.

s Illustrated by R. Ettinghausen, 'Important pieces of Persian Pottery in London Collections', *Ars Islamica*, vol. 2, Ann Arbor, 1935, pp. 54–5, Fig. 15.

[3] Arthur Lane, *Guide to the Collection of Tiles*, London, 1939, Plate 10A.

(1) *Plates* 54–6, *Colour Plate G*; (2) *Plate* 56B, c; (3) *Plate* 56A.

G. *North Persian, from Kubachi; about* 1600. *Diam.* 13⅝ *in.*
Victoria and Albert Museum. (*pages* 80, 81)

Similar bust-portraits of women and men in turbans, and occasionally full-length figures, are painted on plates, which usually have a flattened rim and a narrow foot (1). They are sometimes surrounded by inscribed verses—a feature already found on the black and turquoise 'Kubachi' plates of the fifteenth century. Other dishes are painted with sinuous foliage or animals, often surrounded by scale-pattern borders and shaped radiating panels derived from 'late Ming export' porcelain of the reign of Wan Li (1573–1619) (2). A few polychrome bowls are known, but with one exception in the Musée des Arts Décoratifs no jars, bottles, or other upright shapes appear to have survived. The ware is very brittle and it is only a fortunate chance that has preserved so many pieces unbroken in the houses of Kubachi.

In Persia the 'Kubachi' wares evidently had a wide distribution. Fragments in the Victoria and Albert Museum were found at Īrīn, near Teheran, and a black-painted bowl is said to have come from Samarqand. Professor K. de B. Codrington has shown me fragments found in Afghanistan. Mr. A. U. Pope avers that polychrome fragments 'resembling' the 'Kubachi' ware were found at Sāva, where he believes they were made; but there were apparently no kiln-wasters.[1] A plausible alternative conjecture that the ware was made at Tabrīz remains unconfirmed by positive evidence, and at present we must be content to attribute it to an unidentified centre in north-west Persia. There is no doubt that the black-and-turquoise, blue-and-white, and two classes of polychrome form a coherent series from a single place, extending over the period from about 1460 or earlier until about 1630. Nor is it hard to imagine why it became obsolete. The transfer of the capital to Isfahan in 1598 may have had an adverse effect on industries in the north; but a more sufficient reason was the poor technical quality of the 'Kubachi' ware compared with that of wares developed in other places such as Kirmān. In spite of its defects, the whole series is admirable for the peculiar sensibility and charm of the drawing. It retains a spontaneity lacking in the technically more accomplished wares of the seventeenth century.

Kirmān wares

Contemporary European travellers and the records of the Dutch and British East India Companies unanimously agree that during the

---

[1] A. U. Pope, 'New Findings in Persian Ceramics of the Islamic Period,' *Bulletin of the American Institute of Iranian Art and Archaeology*, vol. 5, 1937, p. 167. Also in *A Survey of Persian Art*, pp. 1654–5.

---

(1) *Plates* 54A, 55B, *Colour Plate G*; (2) *Plates* 54B, 55A.

second half of the seventeenth century much of the best Persian pottery was made at Kirmān. This south-Persian industrial city lies about 250 miles north of Bender 'Abbās, and was thus comparatively well placed for seaborne trade via the Persian Gulf. According to Rochechouart it was still remembered in the nineteenth century as the place where celadon wares were made. On the ground of their distribution Murdoch Smith attributed to Yezd, another Persian city, the wares which Carbonier and later writers have agreed to recognize as products of Kirmān. Conclusive evidence tying them to that centre is admittedly still lacking. It might be supplied by excavation on the ruined site of old Kirmān, which lies outside the present city.

There is no doubt at all that a group of fine Safavid polychrome pottery (1), a large class of blue-and-white (2), and many pieces with celadon and other monochrome glazes (3) are of common origin. A series of vessels painted in black appear to be their eighteenth-century successors (4). The fine white body of all these is relatively soft (though much harder than that of the 'Kubachi' wares); the potting tends to be thick; and the loosely-fitting, rather wavy-looking glaze is hazy with minute bubbles, and has a pronounced green tinge where it lies thickest. Painting on the polychrome and blue-and-white wares is partly or wholly executed in a very strong warm blue, without black outlines. The seventeenth century pieces commonly carry as a mark an imitation Chinese character with a long tail painted in blue (the so-called 'tassel' mark, p. 115, nos. 29–32). An unmarked blue-and-white pilgrim flask bearing the early date 930 H/1523 A.D. (5) shows all the technical characteristics of the whole group. It is, however, not easy to point to many other sixteenth-century pieces that have survived. (But for the pieces preserved at Kubachi, we should have been equally ill-informed about the sixteenth-century 'Kubachi' wares.) The very fine large dish in Plate 66 appears to be the only one of its kind. The outlines of its design were deeply incised in the paste before painting in blue, turquoise, celadon-green and red, the last in small spots on the flowers. On the back is an early version of the 'tassel' mark (p. 115, no. 26). In both design and colouring it bears a family resemblance to the great Isnik polychrome dishes of about 1540–55, which may have been known to the makers; but if, as is by no means certain, the red touches imitate the 'Armenian bole', the dish must post-date the introduction of this colour by the Turkish potters about 1555–60. Other existing polychrome Kirmān pieces all seem to belong to the seventeenth century, and no obviously decadent examples could

(1) *Plates* 57–61, *Colour Plate H*; (2) *Plates* 64–73.
(3) *Plates* 87–9; (4) *Plate* 73; (5) *Plate* 64B.

be plausibly assigned to the eighteenth. The only dated piece, a dish in the Godman Collection (1), was made in 1088 H/1677 A.D.

Compared with the 'Kubachi' wares, the Kirmān polychrome (2) looks remarkably clean and brilliant. The harder glaze and body are relatively free from crackle and staining, and the colours are purer. A good deal of the decoration is in shades of the warm blue, with darker outlines that are taken up and slightly blurred by the glaze—like ink-lines on blotting paper. In fact the ware is strictly speaking only a variety of the Kirmān blue-and-white, with added enrichments, mainly in framed panels, of contrasting designs painted in thick coloured slip. Most conspicuous is a bright tomato-red, very like the 'sealing-wax-red' of the Isnik 'Rhodian' ware. A dull green is evidently the same colour, derived from iron, as was used for the ground of the Kirmān celadon. Through mishap in firing it often changes to a muddy, café-au-lait-brown. A deep chocolate-brown, a thin yellow-ochre, and black are the only other colours used, the last laid as a broad band in the border, and scratched through with white inscriptions or spirals.

The parts of the decoration painted in blue are almost invariably of Chinese origin, taken from late Ming blue-and-white landscapes, foliage with fruit or flowers, borders of lotus-panels and ju-i sceptre-heads, and a background-motive of notched leaves on spiral stems. The polychrome elements are usually inset in shaped panels or placed in alternation with the blue-and-white, with the obvious intention of creating a contrast of design as well as colour. For they are always of 'Persian' character. Commonest are sketchy arabesques and a growth of open red flowers with thin stalks and spiky leaves in green slip which has often misfired to brown (3). Rarer motives are red sprays of leaves, green cypress-trees, peacocks and pheasants, and galloping red gazelles (4). A kalian in the British Museum has a rather tamely drawn version of Khusrau discovering Shīrīn bathing,[1] and another in the Victoria and Albert Museum shows a similar turbaned rider on a red horse pursuing a kylin. The figures are exceptionally outlined in black. Though pleasantly decorative, the designs of the whole group are rather limited and monotonous; and the facile drawing lacks distinction.

The shapes are those found also in the Kirmān blue-and-white and monochrome wares (incidentally, the latter are often not strictly

[1] R. L. Hobson, *Guide to the Islamic Pottery of the Near East*, London, 1932, Fig. 89.

---

(1) *Plate* 60B; (2) *Plates* 57–61, *Colour Plate H*; (3) *Plates* 57, 59B, 60.
(4) *Plates* 58B, 60B, *Colour Plate H*.

monochrome, for their coloured grounds may be painted in white slip with floral and arabesque designs exactly like those on the white-ground polychrome wares). Characteristic are the two forms of *kaliān* (1), and the octagonal bowls, dishes and oblong sweetmeat-trays (2). There are also various bottles and flasks of flattened section whose sides have moulded articulation imitating vessels of metal.

Imitations of Kirmān polychrome ware

A few pieces identical in design with the Kirmān ware are different in material and must have been made elsewhere. They have a drier-looking, more brittle paste, and a thinner glaze; the blue is dull and inky, the blue-painted designs being thinly outlined in black. The red and the green are quite good. A fine dish of this make in the Victoria and Albert Museum has on the back three black-painted marks resembling the letter 'A' (3),[1] which occur also on certain blue-and-white pieces. Elsewhere is a similar dish with sun-faces, dated 1084 H/1673 A.D.[2] One might conjecture that these pieces were made at Zarand in Kirmān province, one of the pottery centres named by Chardin. Alternatively they might have been made at Yezd, which is also in south Persia. It is perhaps some indication of the virtual monopoly of polychrome painting held by Kirmān that potters working elsewhere should have copied it so closely instead of creating an independent polychrome style of their own.

Nineteenth-century polychrome wares

Europe did not become really familiar with Chinese porcelain until the Dutch began importing it in the first half of the seventeenth century. But its popularity caused a revolution in the European faience factories, for the potters one and all abandoned the traditional poly-chrome painting they had inherited from Italian maiolica, and set about imitating Chinese blue-and-white. This fashion, led by Delft in Holland, Frankfurt-on-Main in Germany, and Nevers in France, lasted until the end of the century, when enamel-painted porcelains then imported from China and Japan inspired a return to polychrome painting in a new oriental style. We may compare and contrast this situation with what happened in the Near East. There a Chinese-inspired vogue for blue-and-white set in as early as the end of the fourteenth century and prevailed everywhere for over a hundred

[1] P. 116, no. 37.
[2] G. Migeon, *Exposition des arts musulmans*, Paris, 1903, Plate 49A (Filippo Collection).

---

(1) *Plates 57*A, *Colour Plate H*; (2) *Plates 58, 59*B.
(3) *Plate 61*B.

H. Persian (Kirmān); second half of 17th century. Tassel mark in blue.
Ht. 12½ in. Victoria and Albert Museum. (pages 82–84)

years. But Near-Eastern taste, congenitally more sympathetic to warm colour than Chinese, reasserted itself when political conditions favoured a national revival of the decorative arts. Thus the splendid polychrome wares of Isnik reflected the triumph of Ottoman power in the sixteenth century, being particularly associated with the reign of Suleyman the Magnificent (1520–66). In Persia the polychrome 'Kubachi' wares were also a symptom of vitality, of liberation from the Chinese manner; they were at their best in the reign of Shāh 'Abbās the Great (1587–1629). For the rest of the seventeenth century, under the later Safavids, the Kirmān potters almost alone practised a native polychrome style which was, however, heavily compromised with Chinese blue-and-white. In the troubled eighteenth century even they abandoned polychrome; their latest identifiable wares are in a decadent and retrospective blue-and-white style. The influence of the enamel-painted Chinese porcelain of the reign of K'ang Hsi (1662–1722) and Yung Chêng (1722–36), so potent in Europe, left no trace on the native pottery of Persia. The Persians were perhaps inhibited by their ignorance at that time of the enamel-techniques; more probably their country had become too poor to import much Chinese porcelain, for even the typical K'ang Hsi blue-and-white was little imitated. By the end of the eighteenth century even the material of the Persian wares had becomes seriously defective.

It is mainly this technical deficiency that guides us in assigning to the beginning of the nineteenth century a miscellany of polychrome wares painted in a not unattractive popular style. One small group of plates and bowls (1) is flimsily made of a dry, brittle, paste, indifferently white, with a thin glaze. The painting is in warm blue, purple, chocolate-brown, and pale olive green, with black outlines. The free but naïve drawing shows a characteristic wave-pattern in the border, and pairs of sitting birds, or alternatively pairs of bottles, on a hillock beside growing flowers. We might call this the 'partridge and bottle' family. Other polychrome pieces, of more solid potting with a richer glaze, might be the ancestors of the Teheran 'art pottery' discussed below.

To the second quarter of the nineteenth century belong some polychrome wares that are almost hilariously bad. Examples in the Victoria and Albert Museum are signed 'work of Ibrāhīm'. The thin but hard body is of buff earthenware covered with an opaque white tin-glaze—it is in fact faience. The painting is in a variety of enamel colours—gold-pink or crimson, bright blue, opaque yellow, green, black, and gold—and is evidently inspired by contemporary Chinese porcelain in

---

(1) *Plate* 62A.

a decadent *famille rose* style. It shows butterfly and flower borders in a gold ground, and friezes or panels of figures and buildings in landscape, trying to be Chinese, but often comically Persian in dress or facial type. A large bowl of better quality (1) is signed 'The work of the most miserable 'Alī Akbar of Shīrāz 1262' (=A.D. 1846), and has amusing figure-subjects and real black-browed Persian beauties like the wives of Fath 'Alī Shāh, known to us from large-scale oil-paintings of the period.

A ware of much superior technique appears to have been made at Teheran between 1860 and 1890 and perhaps longer. The material is a good white paste, rather heavy and well fired, with a thick, glassy glaze almost free from crackle. The numerous underglaze colours include warm blue, a pinkish manganese-purple, turquoise, olive-green, shades of brown, and black. An opaque green and opaque pink look suspiciously like the chrome colours used in contemporary Europe. The affected shapes—vases, chalices, bottles, etc.—suggest that this was a decorative 'art pottery', and examples in the Victoria and Albert Museum were actually made for the Paris Exhibition of 1889. They are laboriously painted with flowers in revived Safavid style and signed by the potters Husayn and 'Alī Muhammad. Teheran tiles are still commonly seen in Europe; they are often moulded in relief as well as painted, and show figures in seventeenth-century Persian dress. A turbaned horseman with a falcon is a favourite subject (2); more elaborate are garden-groups and scenes from the Shāh Nāmah. The flat tile in Plate 63B is inscribed 'This is the work of 'Alī Muhammad Isfahānī made in Teheran in the Gate of Shāhzāde 'Abdul 'Azim in the year 1302 (=A.D. 1884). Ordered by Mogharad Khān'.[1]

The Isfahan imitations of Isnik wares have already been mentioned in the chapter on Turkish pottery.[2]

During the nineteenth century a good deal of often excellent peasant pottery was made beyond the River Oxus in Turkestan, which was annexed after 1870 by Russia and is now the Uzbeg Republic of the Soviet Union. The commonest shapes were large plates and dishes, decorated in a style and technique which varied from one centre to another. At Samarqand, Bukhāra, and Rishtan in Ferghana was made

---

[1] 'Alī Muhammad wrote at Murdoch Smith's request a short treatise *On the Manufacture of Modern Kashi Earthenware Tiles and Vases*, published in English, Edinburgh, 1888; also in W. J. Furnivall, *Leadless Decorative Tiles Faience and Mosaic*, Stone, Staffordshire, 1904, p. 215. The nineteenth-century technique closely resembles that described by Abu'l-Qāsim in his treatise of 1301 (see p. 7).

[2] P. 60.

---

(1) *Plate* 62B; (2) *Plate* 63A.

a buff or reddish earthenware with a lead-glaze laid over painting in thick coloured clay slips. The colours, among which a brownish red predominates, oddly recall the Sāmānid pottery made in the same area between the ninth and eleventh centuries; but the bold designs of spotted roundels and stylized plants have no specifically Islamic feeling, so that the wares might easily be mistaken for peasant pottery made somewhere in Central Europe. A second general type is a buff earthenware covered back and front with an opaque, but rather thin tin-glaze, on which rosettes and foliage are painted in pale blue slip with outlines and other details in purple; this is attributed to Kokand. A third class, apparently unlocated, has a buff earthenware body covered with a rather sticky-looking opaque white alkaline glaze containing tin; a bold blue check-pattern appears in the borders round palmettes, spirals, and cross-hatched roundels painted in bright blue, purple and green. Examples of these wares may be seen in the Victoria and Albert Museum and are not uncommon in Western Europe, where their origin is not usually recognized.[1]

[1] There are two unsatisfactory books on these wares: N. Bourdoukoff, *Céramique de l'Asie Centrale*, St. Petersburg, 1904, and F. R. Martin, *Moderne Keramik von Zentralasien*, Stockholm, 1897.

6

LATE PERSIAN BLUE-AND-WHITE

The Chinese prototypes

It is impossible to appreciate the blue-and-white wares which formed so large a part of the output of the Persian potters in the Safavid period without clearly understanding the Chinese porcelains from which their style was derived. These export-wares, which so profoundly influenced the pottery of the world outside China, have been rather neglected by writers intent on the finer types made for the Chinese home market,[1] so a very brief and simplified account of their development may not be out of place here—particularly as the descriptions could stand almost unaltered for the Persian wares themselves. The stages are easiest to follow in the plates and large dishes.

We have already referred to the heavy, wide-based dishes with unglazed feet,[2] which were characteristic of Chinese blue-and-white in the fourteenth and early fifteenth centuries. These robust and useful vessels appear to have been so popular in the Near East that the Chinese continued to make them for export long after their style was out of date at home—perhaps even as late as the beginning of the sixteenth century. As may be seen from many examples in the Topkapu Serai,[3] the colour of these late pieces is relatively poor, and through repetition the old painted designs have lost their vitality. But the mere existence of these late dishes readily explains why, in the first half of the sixteenth century, the Islamic potters continued to repro-

---

[1] Available literature quoted by W. B. Honey, *The Ceramic Wares of China*, etc., London, 1945, pp. 119–21. Also Soame Jenyns, *Ming Pottery and Porcelain*, London, 1953, pp. 116, 122–4; and Nanne Ottema, *Chineesch Ceramiek Handboek*, Amsterdam, 1946, pp. 173–84. The best range of illustrations in E. Zimmermann, *Altchinesische Porzellane im Alten Serai*, Berlin and Leipzig, 1930; and in J. A. Pope, *Chinese Porcelains from the Ardebil Shrine*, Washington, 1956. The last named, an admirable work, repairs all previous deficiencies. It arrived after these pages were written.

[2] Pp. 28–9, 36, 46, 51–2.

[3] One illustrated and discussed by John A. Pope, 'Some blue-and-white in Istanbul,' *Oriental Ceramic Society Transactions*, vol. 26, London, 1950–1, Plate 14, pp. 48–9; others illustrated in *Chinese Porcelains from the Ardebil Shrine*. Washington, 1956, Plates 70–3.

duce a type which by Chinese standards was then old-fashioned. There are even a few Persian imitations of 'fourteenth-century types' which can hardly have been made earlier than the late seventeenth century.

In China itself, tendencies leading away from the fifteenth-century styles in porcelain finally crystallized in the reign of Chia Ching (1522–66) and continued with little change apart from deteriorating quality into the first part of the reign of Wan Li (1573–1619). The typical export dishes of the sixteenth century are much lighter than their predecessors, though still strongly built; they may or may not have a plain narrow flattened rim, with convex sides and a narrow foot glazed underneath. The deep, warm blue does not have the heavily piled, almost three-dimensional effect of that on the earlier pieces, looking more like a flat, limpid wash filling in the dark outlines. An early Ming dish would have a number of contrasting designs, all very carefully worked out, and densely arranged in bands round a central medallion. On a piece of sixteenth-century export porcelain the designs would be less various, far simpler (especially in the borders), and more sparsely spread over the surface, where they would often form a straggle of dark in strong contrast to the predominantly white ground. In fact the several elements are not properly integrated; they may be set each in a medallion by itself; or the same flying crane, long-tailed phoenix, or dragon will be monotonously repeated as often as necessary, with stylized clouds fitted in between merely to fill the space.[1] This sixteenth-century class is richly represented in the Topkapu Serai at Istanbul and at Ardebīl, and many examples were acquired in Persia by Murdoch Smith for the Victoria and Albert Museum. The Istanbul collection has also in store many bowls and dishes of sixteenth-century character, painted in a poor blackish blue, and often bearing a quite unintelligible square mark. This type is practically unknown in European collections. The mark was probably added to satisfy Near Eastern customers, who prized it as a guarantee of quality; we hear that the Dutch in the early seventeenth century specially ordered a mark to be painted on Chinese porcelain which they intended to sell in India;[2] and the Persians habitually put 'Chinese' marks on the blue-and-white they made themselves. There exist pieces of Persian blue-and-white which quite closely imitate recognizable Chia Ching or early Wan Li designs (I),

[1] Honey, *op. cit.*, Plates 96, 97A; Jenyns, *op. cit.*, Plates 86B, 94, 95; Garner, *op. cit.*, Plates 49, 52B, 55; Zimmermann, *op. cit.*, Plates 41–50, 53, 55–60, 62.

[2] T. Volker, *Porcelain and the Dutch East India Company*, Leiden, 1954, pp. 66–7, referring to 1605–10; p. 88, marked cups for Arabia in 1640; p. 130, Japanese marked pieces.

(I) *Plate 74*A, B.

but they are uncommon. Their scarcity may be an indication that they were made in the sixteenth century, little later than their Chinese prototypes, for it is clear that the great bulk of the sixteenth-century Persian wares have failed to survive the wear and tear of time.

A third very large class is the familiar 'late Ming export' porcelain, which may overlap the last in date, but which developed especially in the latter part of the reign of Wan Li (1573–1619).[1] The vessels are very thinly, even flimsily potted, characteristic shapes being the deep, narrow bowls, and plates with a wide, flattened rim and crinkled edge. The dark, often almost black outlines of the drawing are filled with transparent washes in two or more pale tones of greyish or (more rarely) violet-blue. The designs are far more closely integrated than on the preceding Chia Ching sixteenth-century class, and generally leave less of the white ground visible. On dishes the wide border is commonly occupied by a series of radiating, almost square panels containing plant designs, Buddhist symbols and the like; inside this a second lobed border of scale-pattern or lappets surrounds the main picture in the central medallion. Favourite designs are landscapes with growing plants and large flowers, among which are gazelles, birds, or large insects perched on rocks; scenes in vertical perspective with pagodes, water, and distant mountains; and various plants growing in large pots with their roots breaking through below. Borders of white cranes among water-plants or of horses running over waves are common on the bowls. Human figures are relatively scarce. This class of porcelain provided the inspiration for the great majority of the Persian blue-and-white vessels that have survived. Some of these are very close copies of the originals; on others the designs are much simplified, especially on pieces made in the late seventeenth century. Even the garbled designs on the eighteenth-century Persian wares appear often to recall 'late Ming export' porcelain rather than the K'ang Hsi types. 'Late Ming' dishes and bowls were probably made in China up till 1659, when the Dutch carrying-trade from China to the Near East came to an abrupt end. They certainly formed the bulk of the Dutch imports to Europe, where they were still being imitated at Delft until the end of the seventeenth century. No doubt the failure of supplies from China after 1659 gave a great incentive to the Persians to supply imitations for their home market, as well as for the Dutch exporters.[2]

A fourth class of Chinese export porcelain were the so-called 'transitional Ming' wares. These were evidently made concurrently

[1] Honey, *op. cit.*, Plates 97B, 98A; Garner, Plates 56, 57, 58; Jenyns, Plates 96, 97B; Volker, Plates 3–6.
[2] See p. 75.

with the third, 'late Ming export' class, but probably in different factories. A small incense burner in the Riesco collection certainly belongs to the group and bears a date corresponding to 1612;[1] others are dated between 1636 and 1639. Unlike the flimsy 'late Ming export' porcelain, the good white material is massively potted, and the blue has an attractive violet tone. The rather chunky shapes consist of bottles, tall cylindrical 'roll-wagon' vases, and tankards of European form; it is a curious fact that dishes and bowls are almost unknown,[2] these shapes predominating in the complementary 'late Ming export' class. The rather sparse decoration lays particular emphasis on well-drawn human figures in landscape, with cloud-girt mountains and groups of small hooks representing grass. The 'transitional' designs were extremely popular with the European faience factories at Delft, Frankfurt-on-Main, and Nevers. In Persia their influence was much less pronounced; but they suggested some of the human figures that appear on Persian blue-and-white, which also borrowed certain secondary motives. There were 'transitional' pieces among the Chinese wares acquired by Murdoch Smith in Persia.

In 1683 the Chinese kilns at Ching-tê Chên were reorganized by order of the Emperor K'ang Hsi (1662–1722), and a revived export trade brought to Europe great quantities of porcelain in a new style, painted in blue-and-white and in the enamel colours of the *famille verte*. But even before 1683 some rather different K'ang Hsi types were created for the Indian and Near-Eastern markets, notably the robust rimless dishes with a double foot-ring, painted very boldly in blue-and-white and *famille verte* colours with all-over designs of fruit and foliage.[3] So far as can be seen, the influence of the K'ang Hsi porcelains on the Persian potters was very much slighter than that of the earlier Ming and 'transitional' types. No doubt the sketchy character of their designs lent itself less easily to imitation. But there are many rather poor eighteenth-century Persian plates painted with the radiating 'aster' pattern.

The Near-Eastern potters made no attempt to imitate the Chinese enamel-painted vases, which must have been familiar to them throughout the Safavid period; the technique was beyond their resources until the first half of the nineteenth century.

Persian derivatives

There is practically no external evidence to help us in classifying the late Persian blue-and-white. Chardin names five places which

[1] Sir Harry Garner, *Oriental Blue and White*, Plate 55B; later pieces, Plates 60–3.
[2] The rare dishes and bowls, such as Jenyns, Plate 97A, Garner, Plate 63B, form a small group which differ both in colour and design from the typical wares of the class.
[3] Garner, *op. cit.*, Plates 66A, 67; Volker, *op. cit.*, Plates 28, 29.

about 1675 were making the best pottery—*Shīrāz, Meshed, Yezd, Kirmān,* and *Zarand*; he adds that pottery was made everywhere.[1] In 1682 the British East India Company sought to obtain imitations of Chinese wares from *Kirmān* and *Meshed*; the latter lies in Khorassan, at least 940 miles from the port of shipment at Bender 'Abbās, so that its pottery must have been particularly good to make the transport worth while. A ewer of curious shape in the British Museum,[2] dated 1025 H/1616 A.D., bears the name of the maker Mahmūd Mi'mār of Yezd, where it was presumably made; unfortunately it does not help to identify other Yezd wares. We are driven back on the internal evidence of style and technique, and study of the very rich collection of comparative material in the Victoria and Albert Museum prompts certain conclusions. Two groups are outstanding for their excellent quality and distinct character; one is clearly of the same origin as the polychrome wares we have attributed to Kirmān; the other may on much slighter indications be assigned to Meshed. Further groups, of inferior quality, are less clearly defined, and it would be vain to attempt to apportion them among the other three places named by Chardin. With the support of a few dated examples we may assume that the best pieces, which most faithfully reproduce the Chinese originals, are the earliest; and that a consistent simplification or weakening of the 'late Ming export' designs may indicate a date in the second half of the seventeenth century, when Chinese wares of that class had ceased to reach Persia. Wares with a brown edge and dis-integrated blue-and-white designs probably belong to the early eigh-teenth century; after them come even poorer wares in which the blue has deteriorated to a bluish or greenish black. Most pieces bear a pseudo-Chinese mark, and generally speaking each group of wares has its particular form of mark. But occasionally a mark proper to one group is plagiarized on a piece of another, so that the marks here reproduced on pages 115–118 have only a limited value for classification.

The 'Kubachi' group

We have already discussed the black and turquoise and polychrome wares of which so many examples were preserved at Kubachi in Daghestan.[3] The north-west Persian factory which produced them must have made blue-and-white wares in the second half of the fifteenth century, though no recognizable pieces are known with the exception of a large globular ewer in the Victoria and Albert Museum. But there are many heavy dishes of the wide-footed early Ming shape,

[1] See pp. 120, 121.   [2] See p. 99.   [3] Pp. 34–6, 78–81.

which were probably made through most of the sixteenth century. Some come close in design to their Chinese originals (1), having on the back a continuous undulating lotus-wreath round the bulge of the well. These are readily distinguished from the contemporary Isnik imitations of the same Chinese dishes by their crackled glaze, softer material, and very warm, deep blue. The painting on other dishes is far more Persian in feeling. Favourite motives are trees with animals and peacock-like birds, flying or standing with raised tails (2).[1] On a large pear-shaped bottle in the Victoria and Albert Museum the heraldic peacocks flanking a plant are painted in blue with black outlines, and other dishes have interpolated black panels scratched through with spirals. In the late sixteenth or early seventeenth century the heavy dishes are superseded by lighter ones with a narrow foot and the wide flattened rim of the 'late Ming export' porcelains, whose typical radiating panel designs are very carelessly imitated. In the Victoria and Albert Museum is a blue-and-white tomb-slab dated 1035 H/1625–6 A.D., very like the polychrome example of 1037 H/1627–1628 A.D. already mentioned. A few exceptional pieces call for special notice. In the Islamische Abteilung of the Berlin State Museum is an astrological dish of pottery painted with the Signs of the Zodiac and signed 'Made by 'Abd el-Wāhid in the year 971 H/1563–4 A.D.' (3); the painting in blackish blue is untouched by Chinese influence except in the small cloud-scrolls, and compares favourably with that on some of the earliest 'Kubachi' polychrome tiles. The Victoria and Albert Museum has a little rectangular stand painted with a seated lady among foliage, in blue with black outlines. It is in the same style as the 'Kubachi' polychrome portrait-dishes, which are far more interesting and better painted than the 'Kubachi' blue-and-white wares. As already stated, the whole 'Kubachi' series probably came to an end about 1630.

Kirmān wares

Though the 'Kubachi' wares form the only considerable group whose development we can trace through the sixteenth century, it should not be supposed that it was the only fine pottery made in Persia at that time. In the Victoria and Albert Museum is a pilgrim-flask (4) which once had small loop handles flanking a short neck; it is

[1] Arthur Lane, 'The So-called "Kubachi" Wares of Persia,' *Burlington Magazine*, vol. 75, 1939, p. 156, Plate 1, F, G; *Catalogue des anciennes faïences persanes . . . Collection T. B. Whitney*, Paris, 1910, nos. 9–11.

(1) *Plate* 21A; (2) *Plate* 21B.
(3) *Plate* 53A (*not seen by the writer*); (4) *Plate* 64B.

inscribed with a blasphemous poem containing the date 930 H/1523 A.D. twice repeated.[1] The body is of good, fairly hard, white material, and the Persian-style painting of a bird among foliage is in a very bright, warm blue under a thick loosely-fitting glaze which is apt to run into greenish drops. These technical characteristics show that it undoubtedly belongs to the same series as the later polychrome[2] and blue-and-white wares which are reasonably attributed to Kirmān. A second pilgrim-flask in the Hermitage Museum, Leningrad (1), is evidently of the same origin and date; and the side of a third, preserved as a fragment in the Islamische Abteilung, Berlin, is painted in the same style with a peacock among foliage.[3] Probably also of Kirmān origin is an ovoid jar in the collection of M. Clarac in Teheran, which bears a date variously read as 870 H/1476 A.D. or 970 H/1562 A.D.;[4] its shape suggests Persian metalwork rather than Chinese porcelain, and round the sides are growing plants with flowers half-concealed behind long leaves (a mannerism also found on Isnik wares of the mid-sixteenth century). The style of contemporary Isnik (2) is again recalled by the splendid large dish in the Rijksmuseum, Amsterdam, painted in polychrome (3). Here the fantastic flowers growing from a single root owe no strict debt to Chinese porcelain, being derived from the stock of hybrid Persian-Chinese motives that had been current in Persia since Timurid times. Related designs, again un-Chinese, may be seen on two noble Kirmān blue-and-white jars which succeed each other in the second half of the sixteenth century (4). A flask of flattened form in Berlin (5) is impressively decorated on each side with a *kylin*, a Chinese monster that had become acclimatized in the Near East; similar monsters are painted on Isnik tiles of the mid-sixteenth century in the Topkapu Serai at Istanbul. On the Berlin flask, celadon details are added to the blue painting. Very different in feeling is the delicate little dish in Plate 65B, which bears in a

---

[1] Translation published by R. Ettinghausen, 'Important Pieces of Persian Pottery in London collections,' *Ars Islamica*, vol. 2, Ann Arbor, 1935, p. 53.

[2] See pp. 81–3.

[3] Previously regarded as a 'cover'. Professor Kühnel now tells me it is more probably part of a flask like that in the Victoria and Albert Museum, which we recently examined.

[4] Yedda A. Godard, 'Pièces datées de céramique de Kashan,' *Athar e-Iran*, vol. 2, Haarlem, 1937, pp. 334–6, Fig. 153; and Florence Day, in *Ars Islamica*, vol. 8, Ann Arbor, 1941, p. 46, correcting the date. In spite of the fifteenth-century Chinese character of the ornament on the neck, the zones of wide and narrow lotus panels on the body point to a date after 1500. The present writer has not seen the vase.

---

(1) *Plate* 64A; (2) *E.g. Colour Plate C.*
(3) *Plate* 66, *and p.* 82; (4) *Plates* 67, 68A; (5) *Plate* 65A.

double square on the back a six-character mark almost certainly intended to represent that of the Chinese Emperor Hsüan Tê (1426–1435). The drawing of a bird on a rock, however, undoubtedly derives from porcelain of the Wan Li period (1573–1619), and it is probable that the painter had before him one of the archaistic pieces made in that reign. The meander border and the pattern made by the plants indeed recall Hsüan Tê porcelain; the lotus-flowers have, however been tidied into a Persian form with which the painter was more familiar.[1] The drawing of growing plants on the small jar, Plate 65c, with the ground-line treated like overlapping hillocks, again seems to recall a fifteenth-century Chinese rendering of the 'Three Friends', prunus, bamboo, and pine.[2] The quality of the pieces so far mentioned leads one to believe that the lost sixteenth-century Kirmān wares were much finer and more original than their fluently-painted successors. It may be noted that only two of these pieces bear a mark.

Pieces attributable to the seventeenth century (1) almost always have the pseudo-Chinese 'tassel-mark',[3] which on large dishes may be repeated three or four times round the circle enclosed by the foot-ring. The shapes are those also found with the polychrome painting—large dishes, round or octagonal plates and bowls, sweetmeat-trays, jars, bottles and kaliāns. The painted designs are almost exclusively borrowed from Chinese porcelain of the 'late Ming export' and 'transitional' classes; it is only on the polychrome wares that specifically Persian plant-forms and arabesques continue to appear. Under-glaze blue on Persian wares always tends to run—hence the use of black to outline and define the blue patterns on the earliest under-glaze-painted pieces made at Kāshān in the thirteenth century, and also on much seventeenth-century blue-and-white. It is characteristic of Kirmān wares that the outlines are painted in a darker tone of the blue, and are seldom as sharp as the finely pencilled outlines on the 'late Ming export' porcelain itself; the 'Chinese' landscapes especially turn into an almost meaningless blue smudge. Hence the tendency, which soon set in, to simplify the Chinese designs, and at the same time to impart a comfortable Persian roundness to the drawing. Our illustrations (2) show how stylization can proceed until the original meaning of a design is almost lost—one hardly recognizes the Chinese dragon against a wave background in Plate 70B. Human figures are

[1] W. King, 'Persian porcelain,' in *Artibus Asiae*, vol. 1, 1925, pp. 1–3, implies that the material of the little dish is actually porcelain; but this is not so.

[2] Compare Garner, *op. cit.*, Plates 30B, 32A.

[3] See pp. 115–16, where also are some marks that may antedate the 'tassel'.

(1) *Plates* 69–71; (2) *Plates* 69B, 71B, 73.

seldom Persian (1), usually Chinese, an oft-repeated sage with a little boy carrying a standard being taken from 'Ming transitional' ware. There is also a drunken Chinese embracing a wine bottle and showing his legs—this a libellous Persian invention. Quite often the painting on the dishes is supplemented with decoration incised or moulded in relief. The central painted medallion is surrounded by gadrooning like that on the Kirmān monochrome wares, which derive from Chinese celadon; or there is an incised pattern on a white band round the sides of the well (2), an idea for which there is precedent in a few 'late Ming export' plates. The Victoria and Albert Museum has a large dish dated 1057 H/1647 A.D., with a blue-painted rim, a poem incised through black panels in the border, and an incised design of plants entirely filling the centre.[1] Another variant shows designs painted in outline only (3), a procedure found also in some 'late Ming export' and early K'ang Hsi porcelains. The Chinese lady on Plate 71B is from a 'late Ming export' design, but most of the outline-painted Kirmān pieces seem to date from the end of the seventeenth-century, when the painters were growing careless. On a curiously-shaped hanging bowl, Plate 72A, the dancer and tambourine-player are surrounded by foliage painted in the perfunctory manner typical of the early eighteenth century. The break-up of the seventeenth-century style is also shown by the quaint landscape vignettes on a large dish (4) whose black border is incised with a poem and the date 1109 H/1697–1698 A.D.

It is possible to recognize, with decreasing certainty, the stages through which the Kirmān blue-and-white declined in the eighteenth century. To begin with, scrappy excerpts from the earlier designs were painted in a rather pale, watery blue on dishes and bowls which were almost always finished with a brown edge. (A brown dressing was often applied to the edge of Chinese porcelain vessels at this time; it apparently reduced the tendency of the glaze to chip away.) The dishes and bowls were often coloured in solid blue, black or brown monochrome on the reverse. On these brown-edged Kirmān pieces the familiar 'tassel' mark continued alongside some new ones—a group of five or six crosses, a square, and a sign like a capital 'A' with two cross-bars.[2] The 'A' sign is also used as a diaper in the decoration.[3] A much

[1] R. Ettinghausen, 'Important Pieces of Persian Pottery in London Collections,' *Ars Islamica*, vol. 2, 1935, p. 57, Fig. 16.

[2] See p. 116.

[3] Some Chinese pieces also show characters used as a diaper: T. Volker, *Porcelain and the Dutch East India Company*, Leiden, 1954, Plate 7, no. 10.

(1) *Plate* 71; (2) *Plate* 71B.
(3) *Plates* 70B, 71B, 72A; (4) *Plate* 72B.

misshapen bottle with all the characteristics of this late Kirmān class is alleged to have been found at Kāshān, and is claimed by A. U. Pope as a 'waster' from a local kiln.[1] It seems more likely to have been a defective but serviceable piece which passed into use, so that its provenance would not prove anything.

In a further stage of decay of the presumed Kirmān wares, the painting is carried out in bluish or greenish black. Either supplies of the good cobalt had run out, or insufficient care was taken in its preparation. One characteristic design shows arabesque leaves reserved in a ground of tight spirals, like the spirals on the Chinese 'aster pattern' (1). Others are grotesquely garbled, but still recognizable, imitations of the 'late Ming export' designs with panelled borders. Human figures on these are so carelessly painted that the artist has often left the faces blank (2). To judge from the drier paste and inferior glaze on certain pieces painted in greenish black, these might have been made not at Kirmān, but at the unidentified centre (perhaps Yezd) whose blue-and-white and polychrome wares have already been referred to.[2] A tassel-like motive found especially on the greenish black wares derives from the landscape vignettes on the dish of 1697 (3), with the tails much elongated. A new procedure was now adopted in firing. Dishes and bowls were made very thick at the base, and a circular recess was hollowed out on the reverse to lighten the weight; the vessel was then fired on a support which has left three to six large spur-marks inside the foot-ring. Spurs were never used for firing the seventeenth-century Kirmān pottery, but the practice appears to have become general in Persia during the eighteenth century. It no doubt spread from the unidentified centre that made the Safavid lustre-ware.[3]

Meshed wares

Kirmān is the only city of Safavid Persia whose pottery can be identified with a fair degree of certainty. Meshed was merely one of the five places named by Chardin about 1675,[4] but in 1682 the British East India Company evidently regarded it and Kirmān as the two places in Persia where really good imitations of Chinese porcelain

[1] 'A Note on Porcelain in Persia,' *Bulletin of the American Institute of Iranian Art and Archaeology*, vol. 6, New York, 1946, pp. 119–20, Fig. 1. The statement that the material is 'porcelain' is incorrect in so far as it implies hard-paste porcelain of Chinese type.
[2] P. 84. [3] Pp. 102–4.
[4] P. 120. We have also the small vase whose inscription indicates that it was made at Meshed in A.D. 1444, p. 54, as evidence for the earlier existence of factories there.

(1) *Plate 73B*; (2) *Plate 73A*; (3) *Plate 72B*.

could be obtained. The wares of Meshed must still have been recognized in the first half of the nineteenth century, when Rochechouart obtained from there examples which apparently resembled those we are about to describe (I).[1] On the other hand Murdoch Smith (about 1870) found many such pieces round Kāshān, where he cautiously assumed they were made. Carbonier (1899) also gave them to Kāshān, perhaps following Murdoch Smith. But Kāshān was not mentioned for its pottery by Chardin or other seventeenth-century sources, and an attribution to Meshed is here maintained with all due reserve.

The best pieces undoubtedly form a homogeneous class, of excellent technique and design, but it is less certain whether some inferior and later pieces were made in the same kilns. The pure white body is harder and more finely potted than that of Kirmān; the brilliant clear glaze is thin and fits very closely: the designs are sharply defined by fine outlines of intense black, and washed in with shades of transparent blue having a marked violet tinge. There is usually a pseudo-Chinese mark in a double square, laboriously painted in black and perhaps imitated from the garbled marks on a class of sixteenth-century Chinese export-porcelain.[2] Though rounded and somewhat simplified in the Persian way, the designs remain more faithful to their Chinese originals than those on the Kirmān wares; in their clarity and harmonious rhythm they are in fact often much more decorative than the actual Chinese renderings. We gain an impression that the painters did not inherit or acquire a repertory of Persian designs which they could use as alternatives. Some shapes, however, are purely Persian, being perhaps suggested by metalwork.

The earliest surviving pieces appear to be those few which are painted in very deep blue with the flying cranes among clouds and the long-tailed birds among foliage found on porcelain of the reign of Chia Ching (1522–66) (2). They probably date from the second half or end of the sixteenth century. Designs taken from 'late Ming export' ware appear on an unusual squat jar in Berlin, which bears an inscribed date 1037 H/1627 A.D. (3); on a damaged pilgrim-bottle in the British Museum dated 1036 H/1626 A.D.; and on a *kaliān* in the Victoria and Albert Museum dated 1051 H/1641 A.D., of which the shape also is copied from the Chinese (4). We may assume that the ware covers the late sixteenth and seventeenth centuries.

Some significant peculiarities of design may be noted. The human

[1] J. de Rochechouart, *Souvenirs d'un voyage en Perse*, Paris, 1867, pp. 286–8.
[2] P. 89.

(I) *Plates 74–81A*; (2) *Plate 74*.
(3) *Plate 78A*; (4) *Plate 79A*.

figures, though probably intended for Chinese, are incorrectly dressed and sometimes have almost a European look; for example the 'Virgin and Child' here illustrated in Plate 75B, which might have been suggested by a European engraving or painted by an Armenian Christian. The crapulous Chinaman hugging a wine-flask is found here, as on the Kirmān wares. A design of a many-headed monster accompanied by an illegibly inscribed label (1) reached Persia from Europe by way of China; on a Chinese bowl the inscription can be read 'SAPIENTI NIHIL NOVUM'.[1] As at Kirmān, the painted medallions on dishes are occasionally surrounded by a pattern carved with excellent effect in the white paste (2). The varying thickness of line on the jar in Plate 80A recalls a mannerism of the miniaturist of the Riżā-i 'Abbāsī school rather than anything Chinese. The Chinese drinking vessels that were converted in Persia for use as *kaliāns* often took the shape of elephants, phoenixes or toads, but there seem to be no Chinese prototypes for the charming figures of a duck and a lion (3). On a few pieces, probably dating from the second half of the seventeenth century, the designs are moulded in relief before being painted, an example being a flattened flask with a long neck and a huntsman discharging a fowling-piece at a stork.

Yezd and other unidentified seventeenth-century wares

A ewer in the British Museum, shaped like our Plate 75A, is inscribed under the foot and on the opening of the handle 'The work of Mahmūd Mi'mār of Yezd' and 'The decorator of it the poor Zarī 1025' (=A.D. 1616).[2] This might therefore be a piece of Yezd pottery. The body appears harder than that of the presumed Meshed wares; the glassy glaze thicker; and the late Ming designs are painted in a greyish blue with darker (but not black) outlines. The jar in our Plate 82A could be of the same manufacture.

The historian Khwāndamīr (c. 1475–1537) says of a Herāt painter named Mawlānā Ḥājjī Muhammad Naqqāsh, who died in 1507, that 'Several times he made an effort to bake Chinese vessels, and after

---

[1] Basil Gray, 'A Chinese blue and white bowl with western emblems,' *British Museum Quarterly*, vol. XXII (1960), pp. 81–3; pl XXIX. The design appears to have been taken from one of the many European emblem-books of the period.

[2] R. L. Hobson, *Guide to the Islamic Pottery of the Near East*, London, 1932, Fig. 81. 'Mi'mār' means 'architect', and one Kamāl ad-din Mahmūd of Yezd in 1015 H/1606–7 A.D. built (or perhaps only covered with gold) the golden dome of the Sahn-i Kuhna at the Meshed shrine (see L. A. Mayer, *Islamic Architects and their Works*, Geneva, 1956, p. 86; a reference given me by Mr. Ralph Pinder-Wilson). There is thus a possibility that the ewer may have been made at Meshed for the same shrine.

---

(1) *Plate* 81A; (2) *Plates* 76C, 77B, 79B, 80; (3) *Plates* 76A, 77A.

much trial and unremitting effort the form of the vessels he made closely resembled those of China; but the colour and purity of them was not as it ought to have been'.[1] The signature 'Work of Hājjī Muhammad', together with a version of the Chinese 'tassel' mark, is painted in black on the back of the dish in our Plate 81B, and also on a *kaliān* of the Kirmān shape in the Victoria and Albert Museum. These are obviously seventeenth-century pieces, and it is possible that the maker provided them with the 'signature' of an 'old master' to enhance their interest. The material of these pieces is considerably drier and softer than that of the Meshed or Kirmān wares; the glassy glaze is thin, developing a wide crackle; the designs of animals are strongly outlined in black, and some areas are washed in with a rather dirty iron-green, under a uneven, glassy glaze. The ware has affinities with certain polychrome pieces (e.g. Plate 61), whose origin has here been tentatively sought at Yezd or Zarand; and with some blue-and-white pieces with black outlines and the 'tassel' mark in black. We have record of a potter of Yezd named Āgha Malik, who in the late seventeenth century 'was for a long time occupied in making porcelain, in which he had long experience and took the most tremendous pains, so that it resembled the authentic Chinese original in a most remarkable way; but none the less the glaze and colour were not exactly right. . . . His two sons are continuing the profession of their father down to the present' (i.e. early eighteenth century).[2] This account has a suspicious resemblance to the earlier one about Mawlānā Hājjī Muhammad Naqqāsh. There is nothing definite to support a conjecture that the dish in Plate 81B and its kindred were made by Āgha Malik at Yezd, but they certainly have the rather self-conscious air that one would expect in the work of an 'artist potter'.

Unidentified eighteenth- and nineteenth-century wares

The eighteenth-century successors of the typical Meshed wares are less easy to identify than the late products of Kirmān. A small jug in the Godman Collection bearing a date 1109 H/1697–8 A.D.[3] confirms the chronology of a number of small vessels (I) and larger dishes with black-outlined, coarsely-painted excerpts from 'late Ming export' designs. The dishes usually have a pale brown rim, and on the example

[1] T. W. Arnold, *Painting in Islam*, Oxford, 1928, p. 139.

[2] A. U. Pope, *A Survey of Persian Art*, London, 1938, p. 1651, quoting the Ta'rīkh Murfidī III, fol. 208 V°.

[3] *The Godman Collection of Oriental and Spanish Pottery and Glass*, London, 1901, Plate XLVIII, no. 282. Inscribed inside the lip 'Drink water and pray God to curse Yazid 1109'. Shape as our Plate 93B.

(I) *Plate* 83A.

illustrated (1) the brown is also used to wash in parts of the design. Other dishes show birds or animals among foliage, and a large partridge is painted on the pear-shaped bottles. These wares wherever made, have points in common with the early eighteenth-century wares attributed to Kirmān; the brown edge, the recessed hollow under the foot, and the four to six large scars left by the cockspurs on which the dishes were fired. The vessels are relatively soft and light in weight, with a fairly thick glaze tending to form a wide crackle.

Many other eighteenth-century pieces have designs suggested by those on K'ang Hsi porcelain, especially the 'aster pattern'; they are very nondescript and uninteresting. Even poorer is the blue-and-white made in the first quarter of the nineteenth century, an example being a dish in the British Museum dated 1232 H/1817 A.D.;[1] the material has become unpleasantly dry and brittle. A good many bowls and jugs made in this period are decorated not only with painting but also with star-shaped holes pierced in the sides and filled with the transparent glaze; the pierced parts are arranged to form patterns of birds and flowers, as in the example here illustrated (2). This is a survival in popular art of a practice that had begun in Persia as early as the late twelfth century.

It was probably in the second quarter of the nineteenth century that the industrial white earthenware of Staffordshire made its first appearance in the Persian market; its influence on the polychrome Persian wares has already been noted.[2] There is a series of plates and other vessels, said to have been made at Nāyin,[3] whose decoration is alternatively incised through a ground of brown slip, or painted in warm blue; both techniques are sometimes used together (3). The blue floral designs appear to derive in spirit from the Staffordshire blue-printed wares, as does the shape and thin potting of the plates. They are of indifferently white material, with a rather dirty-looking glaze, but their decoration is not unattractive. Examples in the Victoria and Albert Museum and elsewhere bear dates covering the period 1850–80, together with the names of potters such as Muhammad Nasr, Hasan 'Alī, and Mulla 'Alī.

[1] R. L. Hobson, *Guide to the Islamic Pottery of the Near East*, London, 1932, Fig. 86. Bowls in the Victoria and Albert Museum bear dates equivalent to 1813 and 1814.

[2] P. 76.

[3] A. U. Pope, 'New findings in Persian Ceramics of the Islamic Period,' *Bulletin of the American Institute for Iranian Art and Archaeology*, vol. 5, New York, 1937, pp. 168–9, two plates dated 1869 and 1873.

(1) *Plate* 83B; (2) *Plate* 91B; (3) *Plate* 91A.

7

LATE PERSIAN
LUSTRE-PAINTED WARE

One class of late Persian pottery stands quite alone: that painted in metallic gold or copper lustre (1). We might assume that this technique, long cherished by the medieval Islamic potters, had been handed down continuously into Safavid times. But present evidence suggests a clear break in the tradition. In Syria, lustre-painting apparently died out at the end of the fourteenth century. In Persia, a few poorly painted tomb-slabs dated 1481 and 1486 appear to be the last isolated efforts of the once-thriving kilns of Kāshān.[1] We have no lustre-ware that could plausibly be dated in the sixteenth century, for the Safavid pieces, which form a fairly homogeneous group, would not have survived in such relatively large numbers when almost all the other sixteenth century Persian pieces have perished. Their style, in so far as it can be compared with that of the Kirmān polychrome and blue-and-white, suggests a date in the second half of the seventeenth century or even later.

The material of the best pieces is very white, compact, and heavy, being considerably harder than that of the Kirmān wares; the glaze fits closely, but shows a green tinge where it lies thick inside the foot-ring. (A few inferior pieces are softer, and have a thicker and less even greenish glaze.) Bowls of the best quality, and some of the bottles, were fired on cockspurs that leave three small dark scars inside the foot-ring; on inferior pieces the scars are larger and rougher. We have observed that the blue-and-white wares fired on cockspurs are all to be assigned to the eighteenth century on the grounds of their decadent style and technique.[2]

The lustre pigment, which naturally demanded a second firing in a muffle-kiln, usually has a brown or coppery colour, and produces nacreous reflections ranging to violet, warm gold, or rich ruby-red.

[1] P. 33, n. 5.   [2] Pp. 97, 101.

(1) *Plates* 84, 85.
102

Occasionally the colour itself is a deep red, intentionally contrived by special firing-conditions or by an increased content of copper in the pigment. On many pieces a very rich effect is obtained by staining the glaze, which forms the background for the painting, a deep, warm blue. Bowls are commonly blue outside, white inside; and the lobed bottles are divided into vertical panels with grounds alternately blue and white. A deep, muddy turquoise ground is much rarer. Quite often the outlines of panels and some elements of the design are painted in a rather poor blue, as a guide for the placing of the lustre-painted designs to be applied after the first firing; there are even square pseudo-Chinese blue marks, daubed over in lustre. The makers could evidently have made blue-and-white had they wanted to, but if they did, no recognizable examples appear to have survived. They occasionally painted broad designs in another underglaze colour, a bright, opaque pale yellow, with black outlines; this yellow is sometimes supplemented by overglaze painting in lustre.

The shapes have an individual character which differentiates them from the Safavid blue-and-white.[1] The vessels are all rather small, perhaps to conform with the capacity of the muffle-kiln. Very characteristic are the long-necked pear-shaped bottles, and the squat spittoons with a narrow neck and flaring mouth. There are long-spouted ewers with a cup-shaped mouth; 'tulip-vases'; chalice-shaped cups; small coffee-cups; egg-cups, sometimes made in one piece with the stand; dishes, and shallow convex bowls.

Even more *sui generis* is the style of the painted designs. These show no trace of the Chinese influence so pervasive in other Safavid pottery, nor do they retain much of Islamic tradition. They come nearest in spirit to the polychrome designs painted on Kirmān pottery (1), and with their fussy crowding of trivialities seem well on the downward path to popular art. Typical motives are the blossoms and broad leaves of a growing iris-plant (2); the peculiar shield-shaped flower shown on the bottle, Plate 84A; cypress-trees; willows; peacocks; running animals; and something that looks like a very large, hairy worm, but which is intended to represent a stream bordered by plants (3).[2] Inset shaped panels of perfunctorily-drawn arabesques resemble those on the Kirmān polychrome ware.

To conclude from a detailed examination of technique and style,

---

[1] An excellent range of shapes and decoration is illustrated in *The Godman Collection of Oriental and Spanish Pottery and Glass*, London, 1901.

[2] The convention is found on Persian miniature-paintings as early as the fourteenth century.

(1) *Plates* 57–61; (2) *Plate* 85B; (3) *Plate* 84A, *left.*

the Safavid lustre wares that we know must all have been made in the second half of the seventeenth century, perhaps overlapping into the early eighteenth. An unsatisfactory document in this sense is a bottle illustrated by Henry Wallis,[1] with a date that has been variously read 1006 H/1597 A.D.; 1062/1651; or 1084/1673, the last being probably correct. How or where the lustre technique was revived we do not know. Murdoch Smith (about 1870) found more lustre-ware in Kāshān and the neighbourhood than elsewhere, but he was careful to add that there was nothing else to indicate that it was actually made at Kāshān. He found many blue-ground pieces in the districts of Yezd and Kirmān, and compared their material and glaze with those of the black-painted wares found in the same area.[2] In fact the lustre-ware is quite distinct from the Kirmān wares, in spite of certain affinities with them that might indicate a south-Persian origin. The high proportion of wine-bottles might point to Shīrāz, famous for wine, and one of the five places whose pottery was commended by Chardin.

[1] H. Wallis, *Typical Examples of Persian and Oriental Ceramic Art*, vol. 1, London, 1893, Plate 2. The bottle, from the Wallis Collection, has now disappeared. The reading 1084 H/1673 A.D. is that proposed by E. Kühnel. The mark reproduced here, p. 118, no. 53.

[2] R. Murdoch Smith, *Persian Art*, South Kensington Museum, 1873, pp. 22–3. He appears to have been slightly confused through not recognizing the much earlier date of the lustre-painted vessels then recently found in excavations at Rayy.

8

LATE PERSIAN
MONOCHROME WARES

For Chinese celadon there was a perennial demand in the Near East, supplied in turn by the kilns of Yüeh-Chou (ninth-eleventh centuries) and Lung Ch'üan and other places in Chekiang Province (twelfth-sixteenth centuries or later). It was far more difficult to imitate plausibly than white porcelain, and the many Islamic monochrome wares of the twelfth and thirteenth centuries that derived from the carved celadon showed little attempt to reproduce its ambiguous grey-green colour. The typical Islamic transparent or opaque turquoise glazes of that time had an almost cerulean intensity; and they were accompanied by other bright monochrome colours—apple-green, blue, purple, and golden brown.

In the fourteenth century a vastly increased importation of celadon coincided with that sober turn of taste, averse from strong colour, that marked the revival of Persian art under the later Mongol Il-Khans.[1] We have referred to the many imitations of celadon made in Persia and Egypt at that time.[2] It appears that monochromes other than celadon—even plain white—were as much out of fashion during the fourteenth century as polychrome wares. The tone of the green or dull turquoise glazes was deliberately muted on such Persian celadon-imitations as the bowl and dish in Plate 86. But these are still unconvincing: their construction is too flimsy, and the coarse, imperfectly vitrified paste, visible on the unglazed foot-ring and base, is far too light in weight.

These defects were remedied in later Persian 'celadons'. There survive[3] numbers of large dishes so thick, heavy, and dense in substance that they feel almost like the real article; their glaze, now inclining to green, now to olive-brown, is quite deceptive at a distance, though it is soft and easily scratched. Many of these Persian celadon

---

[1] See pp. 3–6.   [2] See p. 9.
[3] Many in the Topkapu Serai Museum, Istanbul (unpublished); others in the Victoria and Albert Museum.

dishes may have been made in the sixteenth century, but some are probably later. We have seen in the polychrome-painted Isnik and 'Kubachi' wares how a taste for bright colours re-emerged during the sixteenth century, after being long eclipsed by the fashion for blue-and-white. The same taste called forth monochrome glazes other than celadon—rich blue, turquoise, emerald, and golden brown. Whatever their colour, these seventeenth-century Persian wares acknowledge their debt to celadon in the shape of the characteristic fluted dishes. But it was a further step from Chinese orthodoxy to apply painted designs to the coloured ground. Even the 'celadon' glazes were thus enriched. And without Chinese precedent, designs were sometimes cut through the colour to show the white of the underlying body. In thus exploiting their materials the Safavid potters showed remarkable virtuosity, and in common with contemporary metal-workers they devised some highly original shapes. It is a matter of taste—*Persicos odi, puer, apparatus*—whether we decry their technique as facile, and their invention as bizarre.

Kirmān monochrome wares

The Kirmān monochromes were quite as distinguished as the Kirmān wares painted in polychrome or blue-and-white. Vessels of similar shape are found in all three classes, notably the faceted bowls and the globular and pear-shaped *kaliāns*. The big fluted dishes appear in monochrome and blue-and-white; both techniques are combined on a dish in the Philadelphia Museum of Art, where the blue-and-white medallion containing a dragon is surrounded by a celadon field.[1] The colouring-matter was applied in the form of a thick slip and covered by the typical loosely-fitting transparent Kirmān glaze. Many pieces (other than celadon) have the usual Kirmān 'tassel' mark, painted in blue. The colour of the celadon-imitations varies according to firing, from brownish olive through pale straw-colour to bluish grey. Upon this coloured ground there are often painted, in thick white slip, the same arabesque panels, growing flowers, and birds on cypress-trees as are found on the Kirmān polychrome wares (1). Details are sometimes added over the white in deep blue, red, or ochre slip. After celadon the favourite colour is a deep, warm blue—a superb colour whose intensity is not matched on any other kind of pottery. This also often has designs painted in white slip (2); on the *kaliān* dated 1049 H/1658–9 A.D. there are touches of yellow-ochre

---

[1] *A Survey of Persian Art*, Plate 802.

(1) *Plate* 87; (2) *Plate* 88.

over the white. Especially pleasing are the pieces with simple arabesque and floral designs cut through the blue slip to show the white body beneath (1). This technique was imitated elsewhere, in the unidentified centre that produced the mainly white wares illustrated in Plates 98–100. The pouring-vessel in Plate 89A might be an early piece of this class; it has a glassier glaze and more compact paste than those usual in Kirmān, and the 'tassel' mark is painted in black instead of the customary blue. A globular Kirmān *kaliān* in the Victoria and Albert Museum is covered with a dull salmon-pink slip upon which are painted white arabesques; but it is difficult to identify as Kirmān productions any of the pieces with yellow-brown and turquoise glazes, which appear to have been made elsewhere. There are a few plain white Kirmān pieces with carved designs, but these are not very satisfactory owing to the rather coarse texture of the glaze and its slightly greenish tinge.

As we have already mentioned, Kirmān dishes and bowls painted in the decadent blue-and-white style of the eighteenth century often have the reverse coloured in monochrome blue, brown, or black (the last scored with radial lines, and washed over with a transparent turquoise glaze). Less certain is the attribution to Kirmān of certain monochrome dishes whose recessed bases and spur-marks also point to an eighteenth-century date. But technical comparison leaves no doubt that the vessels in Plate 90 belong to the Kirmān series. They are covered in coffee-brown slip (the colour used on the rims of the eighteenth-century 'brown-edged' blue-and-white);[1] and the simple-minded designs are cut through to show the white body, with an effect rather like chip-carving. They are to be distinguished from the mid-nineteenth-century wares attributed to Nāyin (2), which have a darker and colder brown slip ground through which designs are incised with a sharp point.

Unidentified wares with polychrome glaze effects

There is one very peculiar group of seventeenth-century wares, quite distinct from those attributed to Kirmān, whose place of origin remains unidentified.[2] Their white or buff material is very soft and light in weight; the very thick coloured glazes also appear soft, and

[1] Pp. 96, 100, 101.
[2] Several monochrome turquoise-glazed pieces in the Victoria and Albert Museum, evidently of the same class, were said by Murdoch Smith to have been made at Susa; but this is unverified.

(1) *Plate* 89B; (2) *Plate* 91A.

must have been fired at a comparatively low temperature. The eccentricities of the ware consist partly in the very bizarre shapes, which have more or less decoration moulded in relief; partly in the strangeness of the colours and their effect when used in combination on a single piece. On the flattened flask, Plate 92A, the panels are moulded with outlines in sharp relief, which keep in separate *cloisons* the pale yellow glaze used on the flowers and the deep purple ground; round the panels is a line in opaque lavender, and the rest of the vessel is glazed in bright opaque turquoise. The technique recalls the so-called *cloisonné* Chinese wares of the Ming dynasty, which may have been known to the makers. The lavender-glazed flask in Plate 93A is made with a horizontal 'tunnel' through the body, enclosed by openwork screens on which the *cloisonné* reliefs are coloured blue, yellow, green and purple. Even more singular are certain long-spouted globular ewers with openwork gadrooning round the sides, and an internal division into an upper chamber for ice and a lower one, filled through a hole at the top of the hollow handle, for the drink.[1] The vein of unbridled fantasy continues in the shape of the turquoise monochrome ewer in Plate 94, and the celadon-glazed jug in Plate 93B; the latter has plant-motives painted in unfired gold. There are jugs of trefoil section, splayed at the base; beetle-shaped 'bath rasps'; and square sweetmeat-bowls, sometimes joined together in groups of three or four. On the sweetmeat-bowls especially the colours can be most odd— lavender outside, pale pink inside, with a splash of treacle-yellow mingling with the pink. (There is a splash of olive-green in the opaque turquoise glaze on the pouring vessel, Plate 92B.) Even the celadon (I) and other monochrome glazes acquire a peculiarly sensuous quality from the whitish flecks and streaks that form within their texture and follow the direction of their downward flow. The effect is unlike that of the Chinese *flambé* glazes, creatures of fire; it suggests liquid confectionery. The vessels were fired either on sharp-pointed cockspurs, which leave marks on the glaze where it runs under the foot-ring; or else on hollow cylinders of thin buff clay, which leave their mark inside the foot-ring. A thin smear of 'golden syrup' glaze was commonly applied under the foot, whatever the colour of the rest of the vessel.

This whole group of pottery invites a curious train of speculation. They are not the wares of the market-place, nor of the ordinary con-

---

[1] R. L. Hobson, *Guide to the Islamic Pottery of the Near East*, London, 1932. Fig. 87 is of this kind, without the openwork gadrooning; the missing spout and hollow handle have been restored in brass.

(I) *Plate* 93B, C.

vivial assembly; they evoke an ambience of soft and secret luxury, an air close with heavy perfume. Were they passed from hand to hand in those hidden chambers at Isfahan, where the ladies of the harem beguiled their tedious vigil with sherbet and loukoums? Did they at his coming, in their ancillary role, catch the eye, and augment the bliss, of him, the Royal voluptuary, in the eclectic pause before fresh rites began?

Monochrome wares with relief-decoration

Isfahan is credited, on doubtful grounds, with the manufacture of a group of wares very different from the last (1). Their white material is extremely hard, and the glazes, for the most part bright emerald-green and orange-brown, are transparent and adhere very closely to the body, covering also the underside. The wares were fired on sharply-pointed cockspurs. The typical shapes are flattened pear-shaped flasks, bottles, and jars, all with rather elaborately moulded pictorial designs, which in many cases recall the miniature-paintings of the Riză-i 'Abbăsī school. A pair of fighting camels, on the flask in Plate 97A, is a subject that had been handled by Bihzăd and other earlier artists; on the reverse is a Chinese monster, a winged cat-like creature among foliage. On another flask (2) a tribesman has in leash a lion—it is too large for a hunting-cheetah; the reverse shows a winged bull (*kylin*) and a winged lion. Both in shape and in design there is a resemblance between this flask and the blue-and-white example in Plate 65A; but in view of the technique this can hardly indicate a common origin. Smaller pieces (3) have equally attractive designs of animals and birds among landscape, and a fragmentary bottle in Berlin shows a standing male figure in the dress of the early seventeenth century. This should confirm the date of this attractive group in the reign of Shăh 'Abbăs I (1587–1629).

Related to it, and perhaps made in the same place, are wares with a somewhat softer buff body, and glassier glazes stained orange-brown, amber, or bottle-green (4). Besides narrow-necked ewers and pilgrim-flasks, there are dishes and wide shallow vessels with faceted sides sloping inwards.

Unidentified fine white wares

A fourth class of Safavid monochrome wares may be easily separated from others in the rich collections at the Victoria and Albert Museum (5). They are made from a pure white material; fine-grained, very

---

(1) *Plates* 96–7; (2) *Plate* 96; (3) *Plate* 97B, C, D.
(4) *Plate* 95; (5) *Plates* 98–100.

translucent, and almost perfectly vitrified; it looks more like white glass than any kind of pottery. The potting is thin; the foot-ring slight and neatly finished; the brilliant, colourless glaze thick and very glassy. To the typical shapes here illustrated there should be added spittoons and rather trivial objects such as egg-cups. The decoration is simple but effective, and designed to enhance the fragile beauty of the white paste. On some pieces the designs are lightly carved or incised, almost disappearing under the glaze (1); on others a charming effect is obtained by means of a blue or pale celadon slip, partly cut away (2). This last technique was probably borrowed from the potters of Kirmān whose familiar pseudo-Chinese 'tassel' mark, here painted in black instead of blue, is imitated on the spouted vessel in Plate 89A. Another technique, used long before by Persian potters of the twelfth and thirteenth centuries, was now revived; patterns were cut right through the walls, to be filled with 'windows' of transparent glaze (3). On the last piece illustrated there are also very simple designs painted in black and a warm pale blue.

Because of its glass-like character, some modern writers have attempted to identify this group with the 'Gombroon ware' incidentally mentioned by Dr. Martin Lister in 1698[1] as 'little else but a total vitrification'. But Gombroon (Bender 'Abbās) was merely the port from which all kinds of Persian pottery was shipped, and we cannot be certain whether Lister had a particular type in mind. The refinement of the ware sets it apart from all others of the Safavid period, and prompts the idea that it is probably of later date—perhaps reflecting the same tendencies as the fragile 'eggshell' porcelain of the reign of Yung Chêng (1722–36), the 'peasant porcelain' of Kutahya in Turkey, and the productions of the new porcelain-factories of Europe. We may recall the statement of von Justi, that Persian 'porcelain' was still brought to Europe in quantity by English and Dutch traders at the time he was writing (1758).[2] These delicate white wares form the only Persian class we know that would have been likely to appeal to sophisticated European taste about the middle of the eighteenth century. Some pieces in the Victoria and Albert Museum, of coarser technique, suggest that the manufacture may have continued till the end of the century or even later. They may even link up with the nineteenth-century white wares, with designs painted in blue or incised through a brown slip, that are traditionally ascribed to Nāyin near Isfahan.[3] Perhaps more diligent search in Persia itself may throw

[1] See p. 76.   [2] See pp. 76, 122.   [3] See pp. 101, 107.

(1) *Plates* 98A, 99A; (2) *Plate* 99B; *perhaps also Plate* 89A.
(3) *Plates* 98B, 100.

further light on this and all the other suggestions made in the last four chapters of this book; an attempt at typological classification of what must be the richest existing collection of Safavid and later Persian pottery, with the barest minimum of documentary support.

9

MARKS

Egypt

Egypt was the only country where Islamic potters habitually signed their wares. 'Signatures' are common on lustre-painted pieces of the Fātimid period (969–1171), but under the Ayyubids (1171–1250) the practice apparently ceased, to be resumed under the Mamluks (1250–1517). The 'signatures' on fourteenth- and fifteenth-century under-glaze-painted wares have been studied, with not very satisfactory results, in specialized works to which the reader is referred.[1] Fouquet gives 23 potters' names, of which 7 are rejected by Abel, who adds 13 names not in Fouquet. The signed vessels are all too fragmentary to permit a convincing analysis of personal styles, and it appears likely that the 'signature' is often the name of a workshop employing several painters through more than one generation. Each 'signature' may appear in a number of forms, often very carelessly written. Only the commonest are reproduced here.

---

[1] D. Fouquet, *Contribution à l'étude de la céramique orientale*, Cairo, 1900. A. Abel, *Gaibī et les grands faïenciers égyptiens d'époque mamlouke* (Musée Arabe du Caire), Cairo, 1930; this is so ill-constructed as to be almost unusable. It is reviewed by M. Jungfleisch, 'A propos d'une publication du Musée de l'Art Arabe: Gaibī,' etc., *Bulletin de l'Institut d'Egypte*, vol. 14, 1932, pp. 257–74.

7

8

9

10

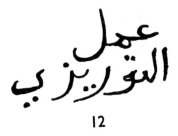

11

12

(1), (2), (3) Marks of Ghaibī, on blue-and-black and blue-and-white.

(4) Ghaibī ash-Shāmī, on blue-and-white.

(5) 'Ajamī.

(6) Ghazāl.

(7) 'Aml (work of) al-Misrī. On the fragment, Plate 16B lower left, is the full signature, 'Aml al-Ustādh al-Misrī.

(8) 'Aml (work of) al-Hormuzī.

(9) 'Aml al-Shā'ir.

(10) 'Aml al-Shāmī.

(11) al-Shāmī.

(12) 'Aml at-Tawrīzī.

TURKEY

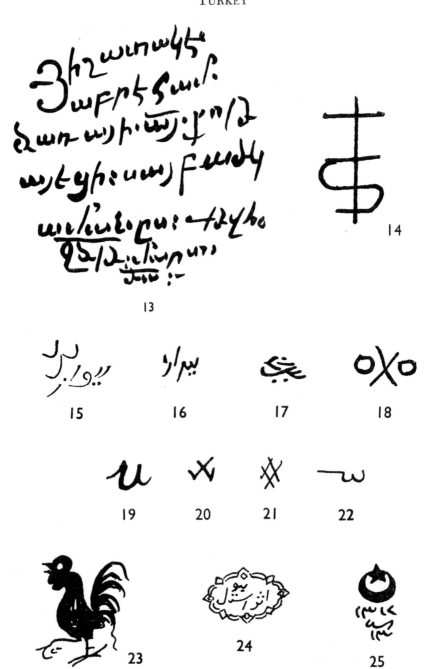

(13) In blue. Armenian inscription, 'This vessel commemorates Abraham of Kutahya, servant of God. In the year 959 (A.D. 1510) on the 11th of March.' On the ewer, Plate 24A.

(14) In black, on four pierced flower vases, as Plate 41A. About 1570–80.

(15, 16) In black. Has been read, 'Siwaz' or 'Iwaz', but may be a mock inscription written by Armenian potters who knew no Turkish script. On Kutahya wares. Eighteenth century.

(17–19) In black, on Kutahya wares. Eighteenth century.

(20, 21) In black, on late eighteenth-century Kutahya coffee-cups. Imitating the crossed-swords mark of the Meissen porcelain-factory.

(22) In black. Mark of Samson of Paris on 'reproductions' of Kutahya and other Near Eastern pottery. The mark is usually omitted.

(23) In blue or black, roughly drawn. Mark of the Cantagalli factory, Florence, on maiolica imitations of Isnik ware made after 1870.

(24) Impressed in the paste, on porcelain. 'Eseri Istanbul' (Products of Istanbul). Second half of the nineteenth century.

(25) Printed in dull green, on porcelain. Yildiz Kiosk factory. Late nineteenth and early twentieth century.

PERSIA, KIRMĀN

26

27

28

29

30

31

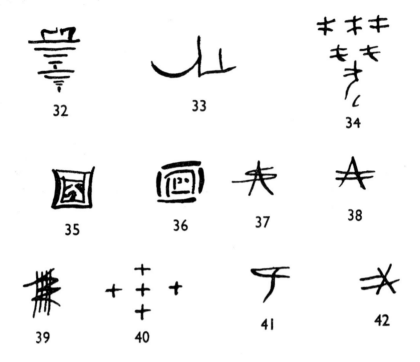

The following marks are always painted in blue, which tends to run.

(26) On the large dish, Plate 66. About 1550–70.

(27) Twice repeated, on a fragment of a very large dish in the Victoria and Albert Museum, painted in blue-and-white with a lion among plants in the same style as the jar, Plate 67. Second half of sixteenth century.

(28) Imitation of a Chinese reign-mark of the Ming dynasty, on the small dish, Plate 65B.

(29–32) Varieties of the typical 'tassel' mark, always painted sketchily in blue. Seventeenth century. The most simplified (e.g. 32) appear to be the latest.

(33) Three times repeated. Seventeenth century.

(34) On the polychrome dish dated 1088 H/1677 A.D. (Plate 60B).

(35) On early eighteenth-century pieces painted with the brown edge.

(36) On an eighteenth-century dish with carved brown slip (Plate 90B).

(37, 38, 39) On pieces painted with the brown edge. Eighteenth century.

(40–42) In black, on black-painted pieces. Eighteenth century.

PERSIA, MESHED

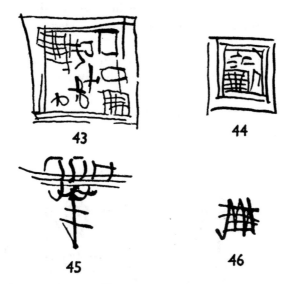

The following marks are all painted in black.

(43, 44) Typical marks of the first half of the seventeenth century.

(45) Probably imitating the Kirmān 'tassel' mark, but painted in black. First half of the seventeenth century.

(46) Four times repeated, on the dish in Plate 78B.

PERSIA, UNKNOWN CENTRE, POSSIBLY YEZD

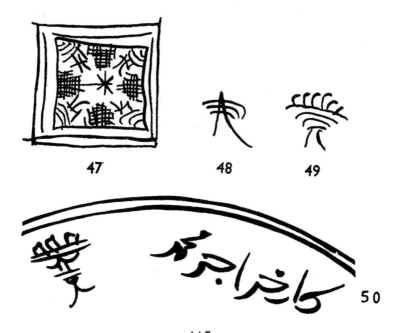

The following marks are all painted in black.

(47) A large sprawling square, on blue-and-white with black out-lines, having a relatively soft body and crackled glaze. Seventeenth century.

(48) Three or more times repeated, on the polychrome dish, Plate 61B, and on blue-and-white. Seventeenth century.

(49) On blue-and-white. Seventeenth century.

(50) 'Tassel' mark and signature 'Work of Khwājū Muhammad', on the dish, Plate 81B. Second half of seventeenth century.

PERSIA, MISCELLANEOUS

(51) In black, common on eighteenth-century wares painted in blue with black outlines.

(52) In black, on a pouring-vessel with carved blue slip (Plate 89A). Probably not Kirmān, as the paste is more compact and the 'tassel' mark painted in black.

(53) In blue. On a bottle with deep blue glaze, painted in gold lustre; formerly in the Henry Wallis Collection but now unlocated. The date has been variously read as 1007 H/1598–9 A.D.; 1062 H/1652 A.D.; and 1084 H/1673–4 A.D., the last being probably correct.

(54) In blue, on the white monochrome bowl, Plate 98B. Wares of this class are hardly ever marked.

APPENDIX

EXTRACTS FROM CONTEMPORARY WRITERS REFERRING TO LATE PERSIAN POTTERY

---

(1) 'Les potiers de faience ceux cy surpassent encor nos ouvriers de Nevers, de Cosne, et d'Orléans, car icy ils la font aussi blanche dedans comme dehors, pointée d'azur de Venise, qui est du verre bleu qui vient de là icy, et ces gens le préparent comme l'azur d'outre mer, en quoy ceux qui ne le cognoissent pas y seroient trompés. De mesme que dans cette poterie cy qui vient de Kirman, là où se faict la meilleure, difficilement la scauroit on distinguer de la tchini. Cette vaisselle de Chine dans laquelle le poison viendroit à bouillir comme ne le pouvant souffrir, ainsi que l'on nous faisoit accroire en France, ce qui est faux, n'a rien de préciput sur ce kirmani, sinon que le kirmani peut s'écailler a l'eau chaude et le tchini luy résiste.'

(Raphael du Mans, *Estat de la Perse en 1660*, published by Ch. Schefer. Paris, 1890, p. 196.)

Note: The body of the Persian wares, white throughout, is contrasted with the tin-glazed earthenware body of the contemporary French faience. The Venetian glassmakers were already supplying European potters and enamellers with colours made up in small cakes of fusible glass, which only needed grinding before use; but the writer is surely wrong in believing that the Persians drew their blue from the same source. The high-grade cobalt mined at Qansar near Kāshān had long been used by potters throughout the Near East, and was also exported to China (see p. 25). It is not clear whether the poison-detecting 'tchini' of which he speaks was celadon only, or whether he understood the term to mean also painted porcelain.

(2) 'Kerman is a large City, which has often been ruin'd by being several times taken and retaken; nor is there anything handsome in it, but only one House and a Garden, upon which the last *Kans* have bestow'd a vast expence to make the place delightful. They make there a sort of Earthen-ware which comes very near to *Porcelan*, and looks as neat and fine.'

(*The Six Voyages of John Baptista Tavernier . . . through Turkey into Persia and the East Indies. Finished in the year 1670*. Made English by J. P(hillips), London, 1678, p. 41.)

119

(3) 'There is also a sort of earthenware made at *Kerman* which is very fine, and being brok'n looks as white within as without. It does not endure heat so well as *Porcellane*, which has this quality, that if you poure never so hot liquor into a *Porcellane* cup, neither the foot nor the brims a-top will be any thing the warmer.'

(Tavernier, *op. cit.*, p. 230.)

Note: Tavernier, *b.* Paris 1605, *d.* Moscow 1686, made his first visit to Persia as a jewel-merchant in 1636, and his last in 1663. He was at Kirmān in 1654. He spent three days at Yezd, but does not mention the pottery made there. The English edition of his *Travels* was contemporary with the first French edition (Paris, 1677–9).

(4) 'La vaisselle d'émail ou de faïence, comme nous l'appelons, est pareillement une de leurs plus belles manufactures. On en fait dans toute la Perse. La plus belle se fait à Chiras, capitale de la Perside, à Metched, capitale de la Bactriane, à Yesd et à Kerman en Caramanie, particulièrement dans un bourg de Caramanie, nommé Zorende. La terre de cette faïence est d'émail pur, tout en dedans qu' en dehors, comme la porcelaine de la Chine; elle a le grain tout aussi fin, et est aussi transparente; ce qui fait que souvent on est si fort trompé a cette porcelaine, qu' on ne sauroit discerner celle de la Chine d'avec celle de Perse. Vous trouverez même quelquefois de cette porcelaine de Perse, qui passe celle de la Chine, tant le vernis est beau et vif; ce que j'entends, non pas de la vieille porcelaine de la Chine, mais de la nouvelle. L'an 1666, un ambassadeur de la compagnie hollandoise, nommé Hubert de Layresse, ayant apporté des présens a la cour, d'une quantité de choses de prix, et, entr'autres, cinquante-six pièces de vieille porcelaine de la Chine; quand le roi vit cette porcelaine, il se mit à rire, demandant avec mépris ce que c'étoit. On dit que les Hollandois mêlent cette porcelaine de Perse avec celle de la Chine, qu'ils transportent en Hollande. Il est certain que les Hollandois ont beaucoup appris en Perse à faire la fayence; et ils y réussiroient encore mieux qu'ils ne font, s'ils avoient là les eaux aussi pures et l'air aussi sec qu'il est en Perse et à la Chine. Les habiles artisans en cette vaisselle d'émail, attribuent à l'eau la beauté de la couleur, comme je l'ai déjà observé, disant qu'il y a des eaux qui dissolvent la peinture, et la font couler, au-lieu qu'il y a des eaux qui la reserrent et la retiennent sans l'étendre. Les pièces a quoi les potiers persans, qu'on appelle *kachipez* (*kachy-pez*) ou *cuiseurs de fayence*, reussissent le mieux, sont les carreaux d'émail, peints et taillés de mauresques. A la vérité, il ne se peut rien voir de plus vif et de plus éclatant en cette sorte d'ouvrage, ni d'un dessin plus égal et plus fin. La porcelaine de Perse résiste au

120

feu; de sorte que, non seulement on fait bouillir l'eau dedans, sans qu'elle casse, mais même on en fait des marmites. Elle est si dure encore, qu'on en fait des mortiers à broyer les couleurs, et d'autres matières, et des moules à balle. La matière de ce bel émail est du verre et de fort petits cailloux de rivière broyés très-menu, avec un peu de terre mêlés ensemble, et le tout fort broyé et pilé. On ne fait point de fayence aux Indes; celle qu'on y consume, y est toute portée, ou de la Perse, ou du Japon, ou de la Chine, et des autres royaumes, entre la Chine et le Pegu. On fait un conte, que les potiers de la ville de Yezde, dans la Caramanie, envoyèrent un jour aux potiers d'Ispahan, comme par défi, un vase de porcelaine, qui tenoit douze livres d'eau, et ne pesoit qu'un gros. Les potiers d'Ispahan leur renvoyèrent un vase de même grandeur et même figure, qui ne tenoit qu'un gros d'eau, et pesoit douze livres.'

(*Voyages du Chevalier Chardin, en Perse, et autres lieux de l'Orient*, edited by L. Langlès, 4 vols., Paris, 1811. Vol. 4, pp. 128–30.)

(5) (In *Description d'Ispahan*, Caravanserai du roi). 'On y vend de la porcelaine de Kirman et de Metched (*Mechehed*), deux grandes villes de la Perse, où l'on fait de la porcelaine si fine, qu'elle peut passer pour être du Japon et de la Chine; car la matière en est d'émail dedans comme dehors: aussi, les Hollandais, a ce qu'on assúre, la mêlent et la font passer avec de la porcelaine de la Chine, qu'ils débitent en Europe.'

(Chardin, *ed. cit.*, vol. 7, p. 403.)

Note on (4) *and* (5): Jean Chardin, *b.* Paris 1643, *d.* Turnham Green near London 1712, was the son of a jeweller and travelled in the same capacity. He was in Persia in 1666, 1669, and 1673–7. In 1681 he settled in England, was promptly knighted by Charles II, and after 1684 went to Holland as ambassador and representative of the British East India Company. Langlès' edition of his *Travels* (1811) includes unaltered the text of the Amsterdam editions (1711) plus the Calvinistic passages which they omit. Chardin knew the writings of previous travellers, but his own observations were exhaustive and appear very reliable.

The 'vieille porcelaine de la Chine' probably means the relatively heavy types of blue-and-white made between the fourteenth century and the reign of Chia Ching, which saw the establishment of the lighter 'late Ming' types. The Dutch would have had difficulty in obtaining any kind of porcelain from China in 1666, their trade having been interrupted.

The Persian potters' belief that the quality of their water benefited the glaze appears to be a superstition without scientific foundation. The description of the ground quartz material is correct as far as it goes, but does not mention the preparation of the frit. Chardin implies that in his time Persian wares were already being exported to the Indies, which presumably includes Indonesia. It would be unwise to assume from a popular story that the potters of Isfahan were known for the clumsiness of their wares.

(6) (Describing a feast given by the Armenians of Julfa in 1674.) 'Pour revenir a notre festin, le service en étoit magnifique, car c'étoit toute vaisselle d'argent ou de porcelaine, qui est beaucoup plus précieuse que l'argent. Il y avoit de la porcelaine verte, dont les grands plats valent de quatre a cinq cents écus.'

(Chardin, *ed. cit.*, vol. 8, pp. 188–9.)

(7) (Describing the magnificence of the court.) 'La cinquième chose est la richesse du service ou de la vaisselle: tout est d'or massif ou de porcelaine, et il y a chez la roi une sorte de porcelaine verte, si précieuse, qu'un seul plat vaut cinq cent écus. On dit que cette porcelaine découvre le poison par un changement de couleur; mais c'est une fable: son prix vient de la beauté de sa matière, et de sa finesse, qui la rend transparente, quoiqu' épaisse de plus de deux écus.'

(Chardin, *ed. cit.*, vol. 5, pp. 479–80.)

Note: 'Porcelaine verte' must be celadon, and Chardin speaks of it as if it were rare in Persia at this time (1674). It is possible that the pieces he saw were of some age, and not recent importations.

(8) 'Eine der leichtesten Arten, Porcelan zu machen, ist diejenige, deren man sich in Persien bedient. Die Materien, die man daselbst dazu nimmt, sind Thon, weisse Kiesel und weisses Glas, welche beyde letzte Materien zu dem zartesten Pulver gemacht werden. Man macht daraus ein Porcelan, welches sowohl an aüsserlicher Schönheit, als auf Anbruchen dem Sinesischen Porcelan vollkommen ahnlich siehet. Dahero die Holländer und Engelländer, die eine grosse Menge davon nach Europa führen, solches allemahl unter dem Namen des Sinesischen verkaufen und man folglich nichts von Persianischem in der Handlung höret. Allein ist es gegen siedend heisse Feuchtigkeit bey weitem nicht, so dauerhaft, als das Sinesische, und daher kommt es, dass das Sinesische Porcelan bei vielen Leuten in üblem Rufe ist, und dem Sächsischen nachgesetzet wird. Allein man kann allemahl versichert seyn, dass wenn ein Porcelangefäss von heisser Feuchtigkeit springt, solches kein Sinesisches, sondern Persianisches ist. Ich weiss auch, dass man in einer Europäischen Fabrike denen Persianern

122

nachgeahmet und Glas zugesetzt hat, als wodurch die Zusammensinterung viel leichter geschiehet und Holz erspahret wird. Allein diese Zusatz schadet ohne zweifel der Güte des Porcelans. Dahingegen könnte dieses Persianische Porcelan allerdings in Europa, sogar von geschickten Töpfern nachgeahmet werden: indem die Anstalten dazu nicht schwer sind. Allein man müsste es auch alsdann in einem geringeren Preise geben, und der Welt wissen lassen, dass man behutsamer damit umzugehen hat, als mit anderm ächten Porcelan'.

(Johann Heinrich Gottlob von Justi, *Vollständige Abhandlung von den Manufakturen und Fabriken*, Copenhagen, 1758, p. 413.)

Note: von Justi correctly recognizes the Persian ware as a 'frit-porcelain' of the same character as that made in some European factories (especially in France and England). It is surprising that he speaks of the Dutch and English merchants as still importing Persian ware and passing it off as Chinese porcelain, as late as the middle of the eighteenth century. For a possible identification of the wares in question, see p. 110.

BIBLIOGRAPHY

Note: Earlier books on Islamic pottery, and they are few, have paid relatively little attention to wares made after 1500. It would not be practicable to name all sources consulted for incidental detail in preparing the present work. Those dealing only with specific points have been quoted in the footnotes, and are omitted from the following list. A few readily accessible history-books are included for background material.

History

P. K. Hitti, *History of the Arabs*, 4th Edition. London, 1956.

Sir Percy Sykes, *A History of Persia*, 2 vols., 3rd Edition. London, 1930.

Sir Henry H. Howorth, *History of the Mongols*, 5 vols. London, 1876–88.

R. Grousset, *L'empire des steppes*. Paris, 1941.

S. Runciman, *A History of the Crusades*, vol. 3, *The Kingdom of Acre*. Cambridge, 1954.

B. Grekov and A. Iakoubovski (transl. F. Thuret), *La Horde d'Or: la domination tartare au XIII et au XIV siècles de la Mer Jaune à la Mer Noire*. Paris, 1939.

B. Spuler, *Die Goldene Horde: die Mongolen in Russland* 1223–1502. Leipzig, 1943.

S. Lane-Poole, *Turkey*. (The Story of the Nations Series.) London, 1888.

M. Brosch, 'The Height of the Ottoman Power' (in *The Cambridge Modern History*, vol. 3. Cambridge, 1904).

General

The Godman Collection of Oriental and Spanish Pottery and Glass. London, 1901.

E. Kühnel, *Islamische Kleinkunst*. Berlin, 1925. Second edition, Berlin, 1963.

G. Migeon, *Manuel d'art musulman: arts plastiques et industriels*, vol. 2. Paris, 1927.

R. L. Hobson, *Guide to the Islamic Pottery of the Near East* (British Museum). London, 1932.

BIBLIOGRAPHY

Editor A. U. Pope, *A Survey of Persian Art*, 5 vols. London and New York, 1938–9. (Sections on later Persian pottery slight and unreliable.)

M. S. Dimand, *A Handbook of Muhammadan Art* (Metropolitan Museum of Art). New York, 1944.

G. Fehérvári, 'The Lands of Islam' (in *World Ceramics*, ed. R. J. Charleston, London, 1968, pp. 87–98).

CHAPTER 1

D. Fouquet, *Contribution à l'étude de la céramique orientale*. Cairo, 1900. (Egyptian wares found at Fustāt; many potters' signatures.)

The Dikran K. Kelekian Collection of Persian and Analogous Potteries. Paris, 1910. (Illustrates many 'Sultānābād' pieces.)

G. Migeon, 'Nouvelles découvertes sur la céramique de Damas' (in *Revue de l'art ancien et moderne*, vol. 44, Paris, 1923, pp. 383–6.) (Fourteenth- and fifteenth-century wares found at Damascus.)

G. Contenau, 'L'Institut Français d'Archéologie et d'Art Musulman de Damas' (in *Syria*, vol. 5, Paris, 1924, p. 105). (Finds at Damascus.)

F. Sarre, *Keramik und andere Kleinfunde der islamischen Zeit von Baalbek*. Berlin and Leipzig, 1925. (Fourteenth-century Syrian wares.)

Aly Bahgat and F. Massoul, *La céramique musulmane de l'Egypte* (Musée Arabe du Caire). Cairo, 1930. (Valuable illustrations for fourteenth century.)

A. Abel, *Gaibi et les grands faïenciers égyptiens d'époque mamlouke* (Musée Arabe du Caire). Cairo, 1930. (Good illustrations, very confused text.)

G. Reitlinger, 'Sultanabad' (in *Oriental Ceramic Society Transactions*, vol. 20, London, 1944–5, pp. 25–34). (Good illustrations, useful text.)

J. G. Ayers, 'Some Wares of the Yüan Dynasty' (in *Oriental Ceramic Society Transactions*, vol. 29. London, 1954–5).

P. J. Riis and V. Poulsen, *Hama Fouilles et Recherches, 1931–1938*. IV, 2: *Les Verreries et Poteries Médiévales*, Copenhagen, 1957.

CHAPTER 2

E. Zimmermann, *Altchinesische Porzellane im Alten Serai* (Meister-werke der Türkischen Museen zu Konstantinopel, vol. 2). Berlin and Leipzig, 1930. (Good illustrations of fourteenth-century celadon and blue-and-white, wrongly dated.)

LATER ISLAMIC POTTERY

G. Reitlinger, 'The Interim Period in Persian Pottery' (in *Ars Islamica*, vol. 5, Ann Arbor, 1938, pp. 155–78). (Illuminating discussion of minor fifteenth-century wares.)

J. A. Pope, *Fourteenth-century Blue-and-White: a Group of Chinese Porcelains in the Topkapu Sarayi Müzesi, Istanbul* (Freer Gallery of Art Occasional Papers, vol. 2, no. 1, Washington, 1952). (An excellent and well-documented study.)

Soame Jenyns, *Ming Pottery and Porcelain*. London, 1952. (Interesting speculations.)

Sir Harry Garner, *Oriental Blue and White*. London, 1954. (Reliable survey, especially fourteenth and fifteenth centuries.)

J. A. Pope, *Chinese Porcelains from the Ardebil Shrine*. Washington, 1956. (Blue-and-white imported to Persia before 1611, very fully illustrated with excellent discussion.)

CHAPTER 3

F. Sarre, *Denkmäler persischer Baukunst*. Berlin, 1901–10, pp. 120–143, Plates 89–109. (Admirable illustrated survey of Seldjuk tilework in Konya.)

Illustrated Catalogue of the Faience of Persia and the Nearer East. Burlington Fine Arts Club, London, 1908. (Fine coloured illustrations of Isnik ware.)

G. Migeon and A. Sakisian, 'Les faïences d'Asie Mineure' (in *Revue de l'art ancien et moderne*, vol. 43, Paris, 1923, pp. 241–52, 353–64; vol. 44, 1923, pp. 125–41). (The first reasoned survey of all Turkish pottery and tiles.)

R. H. Brocklebank, 'Anatolian faience from Kutiyeh' (in *Burlington Magazine*, vol. 60, London, 1932, pp. 246–52). (Kutahya ware.)

Tahsin Chukru, 'Les faïences turques' (in *Oriental Ceramic Society Transactions*, vol. 11, London, 1933–4, pp. 48–61). (About tiles, with new documentation.)

B. Rackham, 'Turkish pottery' (in *Oriental Ceramic Society Transactions*, vol. 12, London, 1934–5, pp. 35–48). (Good brief survey of Isnik wares.)

F. Sarre, 'Die Keramik der islamischen Zeit von Milet' (in *Milet* etc., ed. Th. Wiegand, vol. 3, *Das islamische Milet*. Berlin, 1935, pp. 69–75). (Fourteenth-fifteenth century 'Miletus ware'.)

R. Mayer-Riefstahl, 'Early Turkish Tile-revetments in Edirne' (in *Ars Islamica*, vol. 4. Ann Arbor, 1937, pp. 249–81). (Valuable account of fifteenth-century tilework in Turkey and Syria.)

A. Lane, 'Turkish Peasant-Pottery from Chanak and Kutahia' (in *Connoisseur*, vol. 104. London, 1939, pp. 232–7).

BIBLIOGRAPHY

K. Otto-Dorn, *Das islamische Iznik* (Archäologisches Institut des Deutschen Reiches, Istanbuler Forschungen, vol. 13. Berlin, 1941). (Disappointing excavations at Isnik; unreliable comment on Isnik ware; admirable appendix by R. Anhegger quoting documentary sources.)

O. Aslanapa, 'Osmanlilar Devrinde Kütahya Cinileri' (in *Istanbul Universitesi Edebiyat Fakültesi Yayinlarindan, Sanat Tarihi Enstitüsü*, 5, Istanbul, 1949).

A. Lane, 'The Ottoman Pottery of Isnik' (in *Ars Orientalis*, vol. 2. Ann Arbor, 1956). (Lengthy annotated discussion.)

K. Otto-Dorn, *Türkische Keramik* (Veröffentlichungen der Philosophischen Fakultät der Universität Ankara, no. 119; Schriften des kunsthistorischen Institutes der Universität, no. 1, Ankara, 1957).

B. Rackham, *Islamic Pottery and Italian Maiolica*, London, 1959. (Illustrated catalogue of a private collection especially strong in Isnik wares.)

K. Erdmann, 'Neue Arbeiten zur Türkischen Keramik', *Ars Orientalis*, vol. 5, Ann Arbor, 1963. (Informative notes on K. Otto-Dorn, *Türkische Keramik* and A. Lane, *Later Islamic Pottery*.)

J. Carswell, 'A Minor Group of Late Turkish Pottery' (in *Sanat Tarihi Araştirmala* I, *Istanbul Universitesi Edebiyat Fakültesi, Sanat Tarihi Enstitüsü*, 1965, pp. 1–15).

J. Carswell, *Kütahya Tiles*, Oxford, 1971.

CHAPTERS 4–8

Sir Robert Murdoch Smith, *Persian Art* (South Kensington Museum Art Handbook). London, n.d. about 1870.

Catalogue des anciennes faïences persanes, Damas, Rhodes, et Koubatcha composant la collection T. B. Whitney. Paris, 1910. (Illustrations of 'Kubachi' ware, now in the Musée des Arts Décoratifs, Paris.)

F. Sarre, 'Wechselbeziehungen ostasiatischer und vorderasiatischer Keramik' (in *Ostasiatische Zeitschrift*, vol. 8, Berlin, 1919–20, pp. 337–44). (Important for late Persian blue-and-white.)

B. Rackham, 'Later Persian Pottery' (in *Oriental Ceramic Society Transactions*, vol. 11. London, 1933–4, pp. 73–5). (Distinguishes some of the main groups.)

A. Lane, 'The so-called "Kubachi" wares of Persia' (in *Burlington Magazine*, vol. 75. London, 1939, pp. 156–62).

Y. Brunhammer, 'Céramiques dites de Koubatcha,' *Cahiers de la Céramique et des Arts de Feu*, no. 5, Paris 1956–7, pp. 24–34.

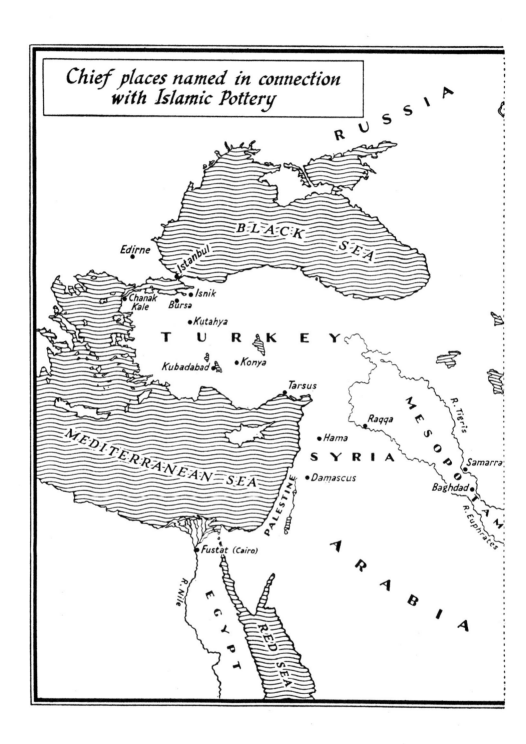

Chief places named in connection
with Islamic Pottery

RUSSIA

BLACK SEA

Edirne

Istanbul

Chanak
Kale
Bursa
Isnik

Kutahya

TURKEY

Kubadabad
Konya

Tarsus

Raqqa

MESOPOTAMIA

R. Tigris

Samarra

Hama

SYRIA

Damascus

Baghdad

R. Euphrates

MEDITERRANEAN SEA

PALESTINE

ARABIA

Fustat (Cairo)

R. Nile

EGYPT

RED SEA

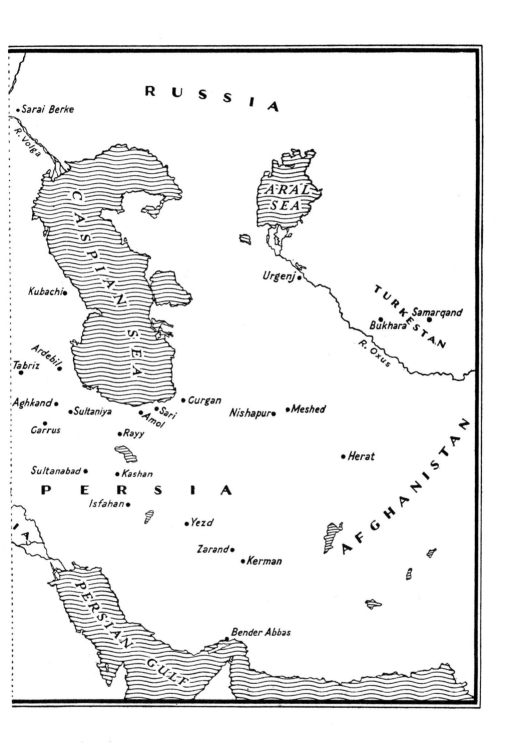

INDEX

'Abd el-Wāhid, signature, 93
Abraham of Kutahya, 44, 114
'Abu'l-Qāsim 'Abdallah, writer, 7
Adrianople, *see* Edirne
Agha Malik, potter, 100
'Ajamī, signature, 112, 113
Alanya, 40
Alara, 40
'Alī Akbar, signature, 86
'Alī ibn-Ilyas 'Alī, painter, 42
'Alī Muhammad, potter and writer, 86
Antalya, 40
Ardebīl, 28, 68, 70
Armenian bole, 57, 80, 82
Armenian potters, 44, 50, 60, 61, 63–5, 99, 115
Athens, 61
Athos, Mount, 60
Ayyubid dynasty, 15

Baalbek, 17
Bender 'Abbās, 75, 76, 92, 110
Blue-and-white porcelain, Chinese, 8, 15, 16, 24–9, 88–91
British East India Company, 75, 76, 92, 121
British trade, 59, 69, 75, 76, 122
Brown rims, 96, 100, 107, 116
Brussa, *see* Bursa
Bukhāra wares, 86
Burgundy, Duke of, 17
Bursa, 38, 41, 42, 45, 48, 49, 53

'Candiana' wares, 60
Cantagalli factory, Florence, 62, 115
Canton, 25
Celadon wares, Chinese, 8–11, 22, 72, 105
  Near Eastern, 9, 105, 106
Chanak Kalé wares, 66
Chardin, J. B., 70, 72, 75, 120–2
Charles V of France, 17
Chatillon-sur-Seine, 61
Chinese designs, 4–7, 9, 11–13, 32, 47, 83, 88–91, 95, 96, 98, 100, 101
  paintings, 5, 6

Ching-tê Chên, 25, 26
Chintamani designs, 52
Choisy-le-Roi, 61
Chü 'an Chou, 25
Cloisonné decoration, 108
Cobalt-ore, 22, 24, 25, 75, 119
Cuerda seca tilework, 42, 43, 54, 62

Damascus wares, 15–19, 29, 30, 62–3
Deck, Théodore, 61
della Valle, P., 70, 71
De Morgan, W., 61
Dome of the Rock, *see* Jerusalem
du Mans, R., 74, 119
Dutch East India Company, 75, 76, 89
Dutch trade, 73, 75, 76, 89, 90, 120, 122

Edirne (Adrianople), 38, 41–3
Egyptian wares, 15, 18–20, 112, 113
European fashions, 69–71, 80, 99
Evliya Celebi, 56, 63

Faenza Museum, 12
Famille rose colours, 76, 86
Florence, Cantagalli factory, 61, 115
Fustāt, 9, 16, 18, 31

Gebze, 44
Gerlach, Stephen, 59
Ghaibī, potter, 19, 31, 112, 113
Ghazāl, potter, 31, 112, 113
Ghāzān Khan, 2, 3, 5
Ghiyāth al-Dīn, painter, 27
Golden Horde, 3, 13–15, 23
Golden Horn, *see* Istanbul
'Gombroon ware', 76, 110

Hājjī Muhammad, signature, 99, 100
Hama, 15, 17, 18, 29
Hasan 'Alī, signature, 101
Hatāyī designs, 47, 52
Herbert, Thomas, 72
Hormuzī, potter, 19, 113
Hsüan Tê, Emperor, 26, 27, 95
Hulagu Khan, 2, 3
Husayn, signature, 86

131

INDEX

Ibn al-Khabbāz, potter, 31
Ibn Battūta, 25
Ibrahim, signature, 85
Ice-containers, 73, 108
Il-Khan dynasty, 2, 32
Illuminated manuscripts, 5, 6, 32, 46
Isfahan wares, 60, 109
Isnik, 40, 44 ff.
Istanbul, Golden Horn, 50
    mosques, 43, 45, 55, 56
    porcelain factories, 66, 67, 115
    Tekfur Serai, tile-factory, 56, 60
    Topkapu Serai, 28, 52, 55
Italian maiolica, 52, 60

Jenghiz Khan, 1
Jerusalem, Armenian potters, 61
    Dome of the Rock, 54, 62
Justi, J. G. von, 76, 122, 123

Kaliān, shape, 72, 73, 84
Kāshān wares, 7, 13, 33, 74, 75, 97,
    98, 104
Khusrau and Shīrīn, 83
Khwājū Kirmāni, manuscript, 32
Khwājū Muhammad, potter, 118
Kirmān wares, 74, 75, 81–4, 93–7,
    106, 107, 115, 116, 119–21
Kokand wares, 87
Konya, 37–40
'Kubachi' wares, 34–6, 71, 78–81, 92,
    93
Kubādābād, 40
Kubilai Khan, 1, 2, 23
Kutahya, 50, 60, 63–5, 115

Lachenal, E., 61
Lajvardina wares, 7, 8
Leningrad, Hermitage Museum, 14,
    94
Lister, M., 76
Lucas, P., 63, 64

Mahmūd Mi'mār of Yezd, signature,
    99
Maiolica, Italian, 52, 60
Malaga wares, 16
Mamluk Sultans, 2, 3, 15
Manises wares, 16, 17
Manissa, 44, 49
Marks, 59, 65, 82, 84, 89, 92, 95, 96,
    106, 107, 110, 112–18
Medici, Piero di Cosimo, 17, 30
Meissen porcelain, imitated, 65, 115
Meshed wares, 34, 74, 75, 97–100,
    117, 120, 121

'Miletus' wares, 40, 41
Miniature-paintings, comparison, 5,
    6, 32, 46, 71, 79, 109
Metal mounts, 59, 72
Metalwork, 45, 46, 73
Minton and Co., 61
Mongols, 1–18
Muhammad Nasr, signature, 101
Mulla 'Alī, signature, 101
Musli, signature, 54
Mustafa, signature, 54

Nāyin, 101, 107, 110

Ottoman dynasty, 38

Padua, 60
Palissy, Bernard, 57
Parvillée, L., 61
Peasant pottery, 86, 87
Piccolpasso, Cipriano, 57
Platter, Thomas, 59

Qansar, 25, 119

Raqqa wares, 15
Rashīd al-Dīn, 3, 5, 7, 12
Rhodes, 44, 60
Rishtan wares, 86
Rizā-i 'Abbāsī, painter, 71, 99, 109
Rūmī designs, 47
Russia, 1, 13–15, 23

Safavid dynasty, 68–71
Samarqand, 33, 34, 86
Samson of Paris, 61, 65, 115
Sarai on the Volga, 1, 3, 7, 13–15
Sava, 34, 35, 81
Saz designs, 58
Seldjuks of Rūm, 37–40
Shāh Abbās the Great, 69, 70
Shāh Rūkh, 27, 33
Shā'ir, potter, 113
Shāmī, potter, 19, 31, 113
Shīrāz, 75, 86, 104, 120
Shu fu wares, 8, 12, 13, 26, 27
Sicily, 17, 30
Silks, 3–5
Staffordshire wares, 76, 101
Sultānābād wares, 7, 8, 10–13, 18, 19
Sultānīya, 3, 10
Susa, 107
Syrian wares, 15–19, 29, 30, 62–3

Tabrīz, 3, 10, 35, 42, 45, 49, 54, 81
Tavernier, J. B., 119, 120

INDEX

1. *Persian 'Sultānābād' jar; first half of 14th century. Black and raised white, on brown-grey slip. Ht. 12 in. Owner unknown. (pages 10–12)*

2. *Persian 'Sultānābād' wares; first half of 14th century. Dark and light blue, turquoise and black*
A. *Bowl. Diam. 6 in. Victoria and Albert Museum*
B. *Dish. Diam. about 12 in. Owner unknown.* (*pages* 10–12)

3. *Persian 'Sultānābād' albarello; first half of 14th century. Dark and light blue, turquoise and black. Ht. 13 in. British Museum. (pages 10–12)*

4. Persian 'Sultānābād' bowl; first half of 14th century. Black and raised white, on brown-grey slip. Diam. 11¾ in. Formerly D. K. Kelekian. (pages 10–12)

5A, B. *Bowl from Sarai Berke (S. Russia); first half of 14th century.
Black, blue, and raised white, on grey slip. Diam. 7⅝ in. Leningrad,
Hermitage Museum. (pages 13, 14)*

6. *Persian (perhaps Kāshān) bowls; first half of 14th century. Dark blue, turquoise and black*
A. *Diam. 8¼ in. Otago Museum, Dunedin, New Zealand*
B. *Diam. 8¼ in. Victoria and Albert Museum. (page 13)*

7. *Syrian (Damascus) jar; second half of 13th century. Yellow lustre on dark blue. Ht. about 12 in. M. le Marquis de Ganay, Paris. (page 16)*

8. *Syrian (Damascus) jar; 14th century. Yellow lustre on dark blue.
From Trapani, Sicily. Ht.* 15½ *in. Victoria and Albert Museum.*
(*page* 16)

9. *Syrian (Damascus) albarello; 14th century. Yellow lustre on dark blue. From Italy. Ht. 14½ in. Miss Godman. (page 16)*

10. *Syrian (Damascus) jar; 14th century. Blue and black. Ht. 16 in.
Victoria and Albert Museum. (page* 17)

11. *Syrian (Damascus) jar; 14th century. Blue and black, with raised white details. Ht. 12 in. Miss Godman. (page* 17)

12. *Syrian (Damascus); 14th century. Blue and black*
A. *Bowl. Diam.* $9\frac{6}{10}$ *in. British Museum*
B. *Jar. Ht.* $4\frac{7}{8}$ *in. Victoria and Albert Museum. (pages 17, 18)*

13. *Syrian (Damascus) blue-and-white*
A. *Dish from Hamā; late 14th century. Damascus Museum*
B. *Tiles from Damascus. About 1425. Width of each 6¾ in.*
Victoria and Albert Museum. (pages 29, 30)

14. *Syrian (Damascus) jar; early 15th century. Blue and white. From Sicily. Ht. 12¼ in. Victoria and Albert Museum. (page 30)*

15. *Syrian (Damascus) albarello; first half of 15th century. Blue-and-white, black on shield. Ht. 14 in. Paris, Musée des Arts Décoratifs.*
(page 30)

16A. *Syrian (Damascus) jar; 15th century. Black and turquoise.*
From Italy. Ht. 13 in.
B. *From Fustāt. Top left, signed al-Ustādh. Bottom left, al-Ustādh*
al-Miṣrī; 14th century. Top right, Ghaibī ash-Shāmī. Bottom right and
centre, Ghaibī. Top centre, unsigned. 15th century. Victoria and
Albert Museum. (pages 19, 30, 113)

17A. *Mosque-lamp signed 'Ibn al-Ghaibī al-Tawrīzī'. Egyptian; 15th century. Black and blue. Metropolitan Museum, New York*
B. *Turkish 'Miletus' bowl; early 15th century. Black and blue. Diam. 11¾ in. Musée du Louvre. (pages 31, 35, 40, 41)*

18. *Persian blue-and-white bowl; early 15th century. Diam. $6\frac{3}{4}$ in. Ashmolean Museum. (page 34)*

19. *Persian blue-and-white bowl; middle of 15th century. Diam. $9\frac{9}{10}$ in.*
Mr. Gerald Reitlinger. (page 34)

20. *North Persian wares from Kubachi; second half of 15th century.*
Black under turquoise glaze
A. *Dated 873H/1468 A.D. Diam. 14⅛ in. Formerly D. K. Kelekian*
B. *Diam. 12⅜ in. Metropolitan Museum, New York.*
(pages 34–36, 78, 79)

21. *North Persian wares from Kubachi; blue-and-white.*
A. *First half of 16th century. Diam.* 15¼ *in.*
B. *Second half of 16th century. Diam.* 12¾ *in.*
Victoria and Albert Museum. (*pages* 34, 36, 79, 93)

22. *Turkish (Isnik) blue-and-white dish; late 15th century. Front and back. Diam. about 17 in. Topkapu Serai, Istanbul.* (pages 44, 46, 47)

23. *Turkish (Isnik) blue-and-white*
A. *Jar; about 1490. Ht.* $9\frac{5}{8}$ *in.*
B, C. *Tiles from Mustafa and Mahmud Turbes, Bursa; early 16th century. Ht.* $4\frac{1}{4}$ *and* $3\frac{1}{4}$ *in. Victoria and Albert Museum. (pages 45–48)*

24. *Turkish (Isnik) blue-and-white; early 16th century.*
A. *Ewer dated 1510 A.D. Ht. 7 in. Miss Godman*
B. *Mosque-lamp. Ht. $8\frac{7}{10}$ in. British Museum.*
(*pages* 44, 45, 47, 48, 50, 114)

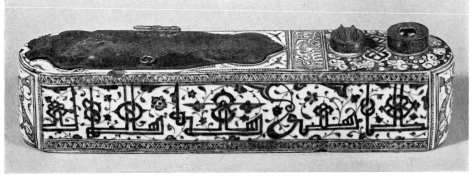

25. *Turkish (Isnik) blue-and-white; early 16th century.*
A. *Mosque-lamp. Ht.* $11\frac{3}{8}$ *in.*
B. *Pen-box. Length* $11\frac{3}{4}$ *in. Miss Godman. (pages 45, 47, 48)*

26. *Turkish (Isnik) blue-and-white standing bowl; early 16th century.*
Diam. 17in. Victoria and Albert Museum. (pages 45, 48)

27. *Turkish (Isnik) standing bowl; about 1525. Blue with turquoise details. Diam. 16$\frac{7}{8}$ in. Ht. 11$\frac{1}{2}$ in. Miss Godman. (page 48)*

28. *Turkish (Isnik)*
A. *Blue-and-white; about* 1520. *Diam.* $17\frac{1}{2}$ *in.*
B. *Blue, turquoise details; about* 1525. *Diam.* 15 *in.*
Victoria and Albert Museum. (page 48)

29. *Turkish (Isnik); about* 1530–5
A. *Blue, touches of sage-green. Ht.* 9⅞ *in. Cincinnati Art Museum*
B. *Blue-and-white. Diam.* 14¾ *in. Metropolitan Museum, New York.*
(*pages* 46, 47, 50)

50. *Turkish (Isnik); about* 1530–40
A. *Blue-and-white. Diam.* 10½ *in.*
B. *Blue and turquoise. Diam.* 13⅜ *in.*
Victoria and Albert Museum. (*pages* 51, 52)

31. *Turkish (Isnik); about 1530–40*
A. *Blue, touches of sage-green. Diam.* 10⅜ *in.*
B. *Blue and turquoise. Diam.* 12⅞ *in.*
Victoria and Albert Museum. (*pages* 51, 52)

32. *Turkish (Isnik); about 1530–40. Blue with turquoise details*
A. *Diam. 9 in. each*
B. *Diam.* 15½ *in. Victoria and Albert Museum.* (*pages* 51, 52)

33. *Turkish (Isnik)*
A. *Blue and turquoise; about 1525–40. Ht. 6$\frac{8}{10}$ in. British Museum*
B. *Painted in thick dark green; about 1540–50. Diam. 14$\frac{1}{2}$ in.*
Victoria and Albert Museum. (page 51)

34. *Turkish (Isnik)*
A. *Blue and turquoise; about* 1530–40. *Ht.* 15½ *in.*
B. *Polychrome; about* 1540–55. *Diam.* 9⅜ *in.*
Victoria and Albert Museum. (*pages* 51, 53)

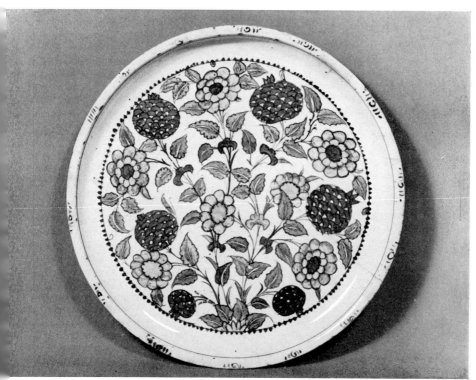

35. *Turkish (Isnik) polychrome; about* 1540–55
A. *Ht.* 10½ *in. Victoria and Albert Museum*
B. *Diam.* 10½ *in. Miss Godman. (page* 53)

36. *Turkish (Isnik) polychrome; about* 1540–55
A. *Diam.* 10¾ *in.*
B. *Diam.* 14½ *in. Victoria and Albert Museum. (page* 53)

37. *Turkish (Isnik) standing bowl; about* 1550. *Polychrome.*
Diam. 16¾ *in. Miss Godman.* (*pages* 48, 51, 53, 56)

38. *Turkish (Isnik) mosque-lamp from the Dome of the Rock. Dated 956H/1549A.D. Blue, turquoise and black. Ht. 15 in. British Museum. (pages 51, 53, 54, 56)*

39. *Turkish (Isnik) lamp from the Suleymaniye Mosque, Istanbul.*
Blue, red, turquoise and black; about 1557. Ht. 19 in.
Victoria and Albert Museum. (page 56)

40. *Turkish (Isnik) polychrome with red*
A. *About 1560–80. Diam. 7¼ in. Miss Godman*
B. *Transitional; about 1555–60. Diam. 14⅛ in.*
Victoria and Albert Museum. (pages 56, 57)

41. *Turkish (Isnik) polychrome with red; about* 1560–80
A. *Ht. 7 in. Miss Godman*
B. *Diam.* 13¾ *in. Victoria and Albert Museum.* (*pages* 56–59, 115)

42. *Turkish (Isnik) polychrome with red; about* 1560–80
A. *Diam.* 9⅛ *in.*
B. *Diam.* 13½ *in. Miss Godman. (pages* 56–58)

43. *Turkish (Isnik) polychrome with red; about* 1560–80
A. *Diam.* 10⅝ *in. J. Acheroff*
B. *Diam.* 11 *in. Miss Godman.* (*pages* 56, 57)

44. *Turkish (Isnik); about* 1570–1600
A. *Salmon ground. Ht.* 11⅞ *in.*
B. *Chocolate ground. Diam.* 11⅞ *in.*
Victoria and Albert Museum. (pages 56–58)

45. *Turkish (Isnik) polychrome with red; about 1570–1600*
A. *Pale blue ground. Ht. 8½ in. Victoria and Albert Museum*
B. *Diam. 14½ in. British Museum. (pages 56–58)*

46. *Turkish (Isnik) polychrome with red*
A. *About 1570–1600. Ht. 7¾ in.*
B. *About 1600–30. Diam. 12 in.*
Victoria and Albert Museum. (pages 56–58)

47. *Turkish (Isnik) polychrome with red*
A. *About 1600–30. Diam. 7 in. Victoria and Albert Museum*
B. *Inscribed in Greek 'Lord, Lord turn not thy face away from us*
May 25 the year 1666'. British Museum. (pages 56, 57, 60)

48. *Syrian (Damascus); second half of 16th century. Green, purple and blue.*
A. *From Damascus. Ht. 10 in.*
Victoria and Albert Museum
B. *Diam. 13 in. Miss Godman. (page 62)*

49. *Turkish (Chanak Kalé); first half of 19th century*
A. *Blue and red painting. Diam.* 12½ *in.*
B. *Purple and brown painting. Diam.* 7⅛ *in.*
Victoria and Albert Museum. (*page* 66)

50. *Turkish (Kutahya) polychrome*
A. *St. Michael. Dated 1719. Diam. 8⅝ in. Victoria and Albert Museum*
B. *Dated 1727. Diam. 4¾ in. Cincinnati Art Museum. (page 64)*

51. *Turkish (Kutahya) polychrome and blue-and-white; 18th century*
A, B. Ht. 7¾ and 8¾ in.
C. Ht. 6⅞ in.
Victoria and Albert Museum. (page 65)

52. *North Persian, from Kubachi*
A. *Black and green; first half of 16th century. Diam.* 13⅞ *in.*
Victoria and Albert Museum
B. *Black and turquoise; about 1600. Diam.* 13¾ *in. Paris,*
Musée des Arts Décoratifs. (pages 36, 78)

53. *North Persian*

A. *Blue and black; dated 1563–4. Berlin, Staatliche Museen, Islamisches Museum*

B. *Polychrome; about 1550. Diam. 12½ in. Victoria and Albert Museum. (pages 79, 93)*

54. *North Persian polychrome, from Kubachi; early 17th century*
A. *Diam.* 10⅝ *in. Dr. Erasmus Barlow*
B. *Diam.* 13½ *in. Victoria and Albert Museum. (pages 80, 81)*

55. *North Persian polychrome, from Kubachi; about* 1600
A. *Diam.* 10¾ *in.*
B. *Diam.* 13 *in. Metropolitan Museum, New York.* (*pages* 80, 81)

56. *North Persian polychrome tiles*
A. *Early 17th century. Ht. 7½ and 6 in.*
B, C. *About 1600. Ht. 10½ in. Victoria and Albert Museum.*
(*pages* 71, 73, 80)

57. *Persian (Kirmān) polychrome; 17th century*
A. *Ht. 6⅛ in.*
B. *Mark, three blue tassels. Diam. 17¼ in.*
Victoria and Albert Museum. (pages 72, 82–84)

58. *Persian (Kirmān) polychrome; 17th century. Marks, blue tassel*
A. *Diam.* 9¾ *in.*
B. *Ht.* 6⅞ *in. Victoria and Albert Museum. (pages 82–84)*

59. *Persian (Kirmān) polychrome; 17th century*
A. *Ht.* 12¼ *in.*
B. *Mark, blue tassel. Diam.* 7¾ *in.*
Victoria and Albert Museum. (pages 82–84)

60. *Persian (Kirmān) polychrome; 17th century*
A. *Diam. 8¾ in. Mark, blue tassel. Victoria and Albert Museum*
B. *Dated 1677. Mark, six blue signs. Diam. 15⅞ in.*
Miss Godman. (pages 82, 83, 116)

61. *Persian polychrome, imitating Kirmān; 17th century*
A. *Diam. 9 in.*
B. *Mark, three black signs. Diam.* 16¼ *in.*
Victoria and Albert Museum. (*pages 82–84, 118*)

62A. *Underglaze polychrome. Persian; early* 19th *century.*
Diam. 7¼ *in.*
62B. *Enamel-painted polychrome. Persian; dated* 1846. *Diam.* 16⅜ *in.*
Victoria and Albert Museum. (*pages* 85, 86)

63. *Persian (Teheran) polychrome tiles*
A. *About* 1860. *Ht.* $7\frac{3}{4}$ *in.*
B. *Made by 'Alī Muhammad Isfahānī in* 1884. *Ht.* $17\frac{1}{2}$ *in.*
Victoria and Albert Museum. (*page* 86)

64. *Persian (Kirmān) blue-and-white pilgrim-flasks*
A. *About 1525. Ht. 9½ in. Hermitage Museum, Leningrad*
B. *Dated 1523. Ht. 9½ in. Victoria and Albert Museum.*
(*pages* 82, 93, 94)

65. *Persian (Kirmān) blue-and-white*
A. *Celadon details; about 1550. Ht. 12⅝ in. Berlin, Kunstgewerbe-Museum*
B. *Square Chinese mark. Diam. 4⅛ in. Late 16th century*
C. *Ht. 2½ in. Victoria and Albert Museum. (pages 94, 95, 116)*

66. *Persian (Kirmān), painted in blue, turquoise, sage-green, and red.*
Blue tassel mark; about 1550–70. Diam. 17 in. Amsterdam,
Rijksmuseum. (pages 82, 94, 116)

67. *Persian (Kirmān) blue-and-white; second half of 16th century.*
Ht. 20½ in. Victoria and Albert Museum. (pages 94, 116)

68. *Persian (Kirmān) blue-and-white; second half of 16th century.*
Ht. 21 in. Victoria and Albert Museum. (page 94)

69. *Persian (Kirmān) blue-and-white; 17th century*
A. *Blue tassel mark. Width* 7⅜ *in.*
B. *Mark, four blue signs. Diam.* 19⅞ *in.*
Victoria and Albert Museum. (page 95)

70. *Persian (Kirmān) blue-and-white; 17th century. Blue tassel marks*
A. *Diam.* $8\frac{3}{4}$ *in.*
B. *Diam.* $10\frac{1}{4}$ *in. Victoria and Albert Museum. (pages 95, 96)*

71. *Persian (Kirmān) blue-and-white; 17th century*
A. *Blue square mark. Ht. 8⅝ in.*
B. *Blue tassel mark. Diam. 10½ in. Victoria and Albert Museum.*
(*pages* 95, 96)

72. *Persian (Kirmān) blue-and-white*
A. *Early 18th century. Diam. 6 in. Victoria and Albert Museum*
B. *Black border. Dated 1697–8. Blue tassel mark. Diam. 17⅕ in.*
British Museum. (pages 96, 97)

73. *Persian (probably Kirmān), painted in black; 18th century*
A. *Diam.* 6¾ *in.*
B. *Inscribed 'Deliver to the sherbet-house'. Diam. 10 in.*
Victoria and Albert Museum. (pages 82, 95, 97)

74. *Persian (Meshed) blue-and-white; about* 1600
A. *Ht.* 7⅜ *in. Victoria and Albert Museum*
B. *Square mark in black. Diam.* 15½ *in. British Museum. (pages* 72, 98)

75. *Persian (Meshed) blue-and-white; early 17th century*
A. *Ht. 9¼ in. Victoria and Albert Museum*
B. *Square mark in black. Dated 1627. Berlin, Staatliche Museen,
Islamisches Museum. (pages 73, 98, 99)*

76. *Persian (Meshed) blue-and-white; first half of 17th century*
A. *Ht. 5⅞ in. Victoria and Albert Museum*
B. *Ht. 5¾ in. British Museum*
C. *Square mark in black. Diam. 20 in. Victoria and Albert Museum.*
(pages 73, 98, 99)

77. *Persian (Meshed) blue-and-white; first half of 17th century*
A. *Length 6 in.*
B. *Square mark in black. Diam. 18¼ in. Victoria and Albert Museum.*
(pages 73, 98, 99)

78. *Persian (Meshed) blue-and-white; first half of 17th century.*
Black square marks
A. *Dated 1627. Berlin, Staatliche Museen*
B. *Diam.* 17½ *in. Victoria and Albert Museum.* (*pages* 98, 117)

79. *Persian (Meshed) blue-and-white; first half of 17th century*
A. *Dated 1641. Ht. 7 in.*
B. *Black square mark. Diam. 17⅝ in. Victoria and Albert Museum.*
(pages 73, 98, 99)

80. *Persian (Meshed) blue-and-white; first half of 17th century*
A. *Ht. 11⅝ in.*
B. *Black square mark. Diam. 14¾ in. Victoria and Albert Museum.*
(pages 98, 99)

81. *Persian blue-and-white; second half of 17th century*
A. *Meshed. Black square mark. Diam.* 17⅞ *in.*
B. *Signed 'Ḥājjī Muḥammad'. Details in green and black. Diam.* 17⅞ *in.*
Victoria and Albert Museum. (*pages* 98, 99, 100, 118)

82. *Persian blue-and-white*
A. *First half of 17th century. Ht.* $7\frac{1}{4}$ *in.*
B. *18th century. Brown edge, mark a black sign. Diam.* $9\frac{5}{8}$ *in.*
Victoria and Albert Museum. (*pages* 100, 101)

83. *Persian blue-and-white; 18th century*
A. *Width* 5⅝ *in.*
B. *Details in brown. Diam.* 14⅜ *in. Victoria and Albert Museum.*
(*pages* 100, 101)

84. *Persian, painted in lustre; second half of 17th century*
A. *Ht.* 10½ *in. Victoria and Albert Museum*
B. *Diam. 9 in. Charles Kelekian, New York.* (*pages* 102, 103)

85. *Persian, painted in lustre; second half of 17th century*
A. *Ht. 10¼ in. Victoria and Albert Museum*
B. *Blue ground. Signed 'Hātim'. Ht. 5$\frac{7}{10}$ in. British Museum*
(pages 73, 102, 103)

86. *Persian, with celadon glaze; first half of* 14*th century*
A. *From Sultaniya. Diam.* 5⅝ *in.*
B. *Diam.* 13¾ *in. Victoria and Albert Museum.* (*page* 105)

87. *Persian (Kirmān), with celadon ground, painted in white, blue and
red*
A. *Ht. 6½ in.*
B. *Diam. 10¼ in. Victoria and Albert Museum. (pages 72, 82, 106)*

88. *Persian (Kirmān), with blue ground painted in white;*
17th century
A. *Diam.* 5½ *in.*
B. *Dated 1658–9. Touches of yellow ochre. Ht.* 11½ *in.*
Victoria and Albert Museum. (pages 73, 106)

89. *Persian, with blue ground cut through; 17th century*
A. *Mark, tassel in black. Ht.* $4\frac{1}{4}$ *in.*
B. *Kirmān. Mark, tassel in blue. Diam. 10 in.*
Victoria and Albert Museum. (pages 107, 110, 118)

90. *Persian (Kirmān), with brown ground cut through; 18th century*
A. *Ht.* $5\frac{1}{8}$ *in.*
B. *Square mark in blue. Diam.* $9\frac{1}{8}$ *in.*
Victoria and Albert Museum. (*pages* 107, 116)

91. *Persian wares*
A. *Brown ground cut through, signed 'Muhammad Nasr'. Nāyin;*
1864–5. Diam. 10 in.
B. *Blue-and-white, dated 1809. Diam. $8\frac{7}{8}$ in.*
Victoria and Albert Museum. (pages 101, 107)

92. *Persian, with coloured glazes; 17th century*
A. *Turquoise, lavender, purple and yellow. Ht. 12 in.*
B. *Turquoise. Ht. 5¼ in. Victoria and Albert Museum.*
(pages 71, 73, 108)

93. *Persian, with coloured glazes; first half of 17th century*
A. *Lavender, blue, green, yellow and purple. Ht. 7 in.*
B. *Grey-green, with unfired gold. Ht. 8½ in.*
C. *Grey-green. Ht. 7½ in. Victoria and Albert Museum. (pages* 71, 108)

94. *Persian, with opaque turquoise glaze; first half of* 17th *century
Ht.* $10\frac{3}{4}$ *in. Victoria and Albert Museum.* (*pages* 71, 108)

95. *Persian, with amber glaze; first half of* 17th *century. Ht.* $11\frac{1}{2}$ *in.*
Victoria and Albert Museum. (*page* 109)

96. *Persian, with green glaze; early 17th century. Ht. 14¾ in.*
Victoria and Albert Museum. (pages 71, 109)

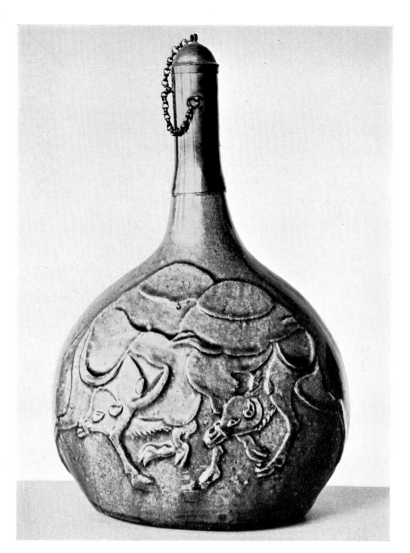

97. *Persian monochromes; early 17th century*
A. *Green. Ht.* 9½ *in.*
B. *Amber. Ht.* 4 *in.*
C, D. *Green. Victoria and Albert Museum.* (*pages* 71, 109)

98. *Persian white wares; second half of* 17*th century or later*
A. *Ht.* 5⅞ *in.*
B. *Mark, four blue crosses. Diam.* 6¾ *in. Victoria and Albert Museum.*
(*pages* 109, 110, 118)

99. *Persian; second half of 17th century or later.*
A. *White. Diam. 9 in.*
B. *Grey-green cut through, on white. Diam. $8\frac{1}{4}$ in.*
Victoria and Albert Museum. (*pages* 109, 110)

100. *Persian pierced ware painted in black and blue; second half of
17th century or later*
A. *Diam. 8 in.*
B. *Diam.* $8\frac{1}{2}$ *in. Victoria and Albert Museum. (pages* 109, 110)